Terri Psiakis has top-s
stand-up comic, writer
she has appeared on *Rove*, *The Glass House*, *Spicks and Specks*, ABC TV's *Stand Up!* and The Comedy Channel's *Stand Up Australia*. She has written and performed six shows for the Melbourne International Comedy Festival and has toured the nation with the Comedy Festival Roadshow. She will also be familiar to listeners of national youth broadcaster Triple J, where she was a regular presenter for six years.

Terri now co-hosts her own Triple M weekend breakfast show, 'Toast', with Justin Hamilton and Charlie Pickering.

Typically, Terri likes taking long walks on the beach. She also enjoys hiding out in her little house in the suburbs with her giant beagle and her beloved Bloke.

TYING
THE
KNOT

without doing your block

TERRI PSIAKIS

EBURY
PRESS

An Ebury Press book
Published by Random House Australia Pty Ltd
Level 3, 100 Pacific Highway, North Sydney NSW 2060
www.randomhouse.com.au

First published by Ebury Press in 2009

Addresses for companies within the Random House Group can be found at www.randomhouse.com.au/offices

National Library of Australia
Cataloguing-in-Publication Entry

Psiakis, Terri.
Tying the knot without doing your block.

ISBN 978 1 74166 885 8 (pbk).

Psiakis, Terri.
Weddings – Planning.
Wedding etiquette.
Women comedians – Australia – Biography.

395.22

Internal wedding photography by Robyn Slavin Photography
Cover and internal design by Christabella Designs
Typeset in Minion 12/16 pt by Midland Typesetters, Australia
Printed and bound by Griffin Press, South Australia

To my husband
with love, gratitude and bacon

and also

To my parents
with love, thanks and admiration

CONTENTS

INTRODUCTION

LADY

Dear Soon-To-Be-Married Lady,

Congratulations! Welcome to planning your wedding. I don't know how far into the planning process you are so let's take stock for a moment and find out how you're feeling:

On the verge of tears? Go straight to page 291. Then come back here when you're done.

Feeling tops? Good to hear. A glass of bubbly for the lady with the big, shiny smile!

Shitting yourself? Please relax (and no, I can't believe I said 'shit' on the first page either). Some people freak out when it comes to wedding planning but my little book contains nothing to fear.

Have a nip of something Irish and keep reading. I'm serious.

I got hitched on Sunday, 25th of May 2008, and I can honestly tell you it was the best day of my life. And I wasn't even drunk! (The more astute among you are probably picking up on a theme.)

The thing is, not only was the actual wedding fun but I really, really enjoyed all the planning. And that surprised me a little because I'd expected it to be stressful. This was partly due to the fact that for some reason, whenever I told another married person I was planning my wedding, they'd always roll their eyes towards the heavens, then put a hand on my shoulder and in a really low voice, ask if I was okay. And the other reason I expected it to be stressful was because every wedding planning guide I picked up kind of made a little bit of vomit come up into my mouth.

You see, most wedding guides are pretty much all the same: they're very girly, very fussy and very traditional. They take everything way too seriously. And not one of them contains the phrase 'Let's all have a drink!'

On the other hand, my little book is, quite simply, from me to you. And here's what you need to know about me: I am not a girly-girl. I don't believe in frills and frou-frou. I like doing things my own way. And I can smell a load of crap a mile off.

All that came into play when I was planning my

wedding. And most importantly, it all comes into play in this book. Here's the deal: I promise to tell you the truth, the whole truth and nothing but the truth about wedding planning. Although I should point out I'm not a trained expert. I'm not a professional wedding planner or a fancy-pants events coordinator. I'm just a comedian who got married, so anything I say is based solely on my own opinion and experience.

There are even sections for your Almost-Husband: they're called Bloke's World (because I'm creative) and they pop up throughout the book. Most wedding guides don't offer anything to people with testicles and I've always thought that's a bit strange. It's their wedding too, so I've included stuff for them in this book – they've got their own introduction and everything.

But if your bloke's anything like mine, it's hard to get him to read anything that doesn't involve nudity or sport (or even better, nude sport). So here's my advice: once you've read this book, bookmark the Bloke's World sections and leave the book in the bathroom for your Almost-Husband to read on the bog. Then promise him that once he's done reading, you'll play kick-to-kick with your top off. Trust me, this works. Don't ask me how I know.

As well as advice and suggestions, I'll also tell you some stories about events and situations that happened to me. In fact, I'd love for you to think of this book as both a reference and a source of enter-tainment. Because God knows weddings can bring out the weird-arses (see The Celebrant, page 147).

Oh, and while we're on the subject of this book being a reference, there's something else you should probably know. I'm not a real go-getter. In fact, sometimes I really like being half-arsed. (Just ask my editor – you wouldn't know it to look at her now, but she never even used to drink.) To put it bluntly, throughout the process of planning my wedding there were plenty of things I just couldn't care less about. So while this book will certainly help you, it's not a detailed encyclopedia. Think of it more along the lines of a guide to how to plan a wedding without really trying. No, really.

I hope *Tying the Knot Without Doing Your Block* makes you laugh while you plan your wedding.

Now, let's all have a drink!

INTRODUCTION

BLOKE

Dear Soon-To-Be-Married Bloke,

Congratulations! Welcome to your bog. I'm assuming you're reading this book on the toilet because your Nearly-Wife has left it here for you. She's pretty clever, isn't she? Taught her everything I know.

I hope you don't feel any less testicular for reading a book about weddings, but think of it this way: unless you're in the habit of bringing your mates to the bog for moral support, none of them will ever know about this. (Although come to think of it, we all know what it's like when you go too hard on a green curry, so if you're really worried, just hide this book inside a copy of *Ralph*.)

The fact is, this is totally your wedding (not right here in the bog, but generally speaking). And contrary to popular belief, the day is just as much about you as it is about the beautiful woman you'll be sharing it with. I know that since you got engaged everyone's probably made more of a fuss over your Nearly-Wife – what's she going to wear? How's she going to have her hair? When's she going to get pregnant? (Okay, the last one might just be peculiar to my family.) But trust me, that doesn't give this occasion any less importance for you. There are a few things you're going to have to think about as well. And that's where you're going to need me and this book.

Quick introduction: Hi, I'm not a professional. I'm just a comedian who got hitched on the 25th of May 2008. I don't want to exaggerate but it was the best day ever in the history of the whole world. And I'd like use the knowledge and experience I gained from planning my celebration to help you make your wedding just as good. Promise.

This is a book about wedding planning and, while most of it's directed at your Nearly-Wife (let's face it, you and I both know she wears the pants in the planning department), there are some bits I'm directing solely at you. You'll find them in the Bloke's World sections your Nearly-Wife has probably already bookmarked for you. Read them. Learn from and be inspired by them. I guarantee they will make planning your wedding easier.

The fact is, you don't have to worry about as many planning details as your Nearly-Wife does but there are some things I know you'd like to have a say in. For example, if you're like my Bloke, you probably don't give a stuff about the floral arrangements but you'd give your left nut to have a rack of lamb on the dinner menu at the reception.* The

---

* Please note that despite this delightful turn of phrase, no nuts were harmed in the planning of my wedding.

Bloke's World sections of this book will help you achieve that goal and others, as well as ensuring the following:

1. Your Nearly-Wife doesn't spend most of the planning process in tears. Or nagging you. Or tearfully nagging you while simultaneously threatening to cut off your supply of sex, which she has made considerably more frequent since you proposed. Yeah. You know what I'm talking about.

2. Your in-laws don't have a crack at you for spending the planning process doing fuck-all while their daughter quietly does her block (these are all technical terms that in-laws often use when they're thinking about trying to talk their daughter out of marrying someone).

3. You're able to look back on your wedding with the pride and satisfaction that comes with knowing you helped plan the most important day of your life so far … and it all turned out better than boobs.

So that's what the Bloke's World sections of this book have in store for you, although you're also welcome to read whichever other bits take your fancy. You might want to check out the funny stories in here about stuff that happened to me and my Bloke. If your Nearly-Wife's been a bit of a stress-head lately, you might want to brush up on the details of Cocktails, page 291. What you gain from this book will only be limited by the amount of time you can spend on the bog before your bum goes numb.

Enjoy!

PART

oNE

In the beginning...

How I Met The Bloke

(or why not all corporate gigs suck)

In 2005 I performed a Melbourne International Comedy Festival show about being single, but it was a show about being single and happy as opposed to being single and rocking backwards and forwards in a corner, quietly humming 'Not Pretty Enough'.

That show was called *Available* but I didn't choose the title – my dad came up with it. He was convinced that if he let everyone know I was available on a poster he'd be able to marry me off by the end of the festival. My own dad was pimping me out, which I would have been totally outraged about if only it hadn't worked.

Basically, what happened was this: the festival finished and I was still single at the end of it. But about a month later I was booked to do a gig at a corporate function. Most comedians will tell you that corporate gigs – how can I put this delicately? – suck the big one. They pay well but you're usually performing to people in suits who are thinking: 'I didn't ask for this. Who's responsible for this? Was it Gary from marketing?' Either that or they're all really drunk.

I'm not kidding. I once did a gig for a bunch of midwives. And I know what you're thinking: 'Come on, Tez. Midwives are pretty cool, calm and collected. Surely that was an easy gig.' And you're right: midwives are cool, calm and collected – when they're at work. But when you give 342 midwives access to an open bar, it's a different story. Some of those midwives got so drunk they were trying to deliver babies that hadn't even been conceived yet. (Don't think about that for too long.)

At my first ever corporate gig, the first question they asked me was 'Did you bring your own microphone?' It went downhill from there. At another, they started serving lunch from a bain-marie ten minutes into my half-hour set. The entire audience got up to join the lunch queue and there they stood, mostly with their backs to me, while I tried to figure out why I'd ever been born.

After a corporate gig attended by very wealthy, well-to-do women where I did material about living in suburban Watsonia, a woman approached me at dinner to ask 'Do you *really* live there? It's funny – sometimes I get so used to living in (insert name of hoity-toity locale here) that I forget suburbs like yours even *exist*.' In retrospect, maybe I should have chosen different material. In retrospect, I'm also glad I wasn't carrying a gun.

At a corporate function hosted by a Channel Nine weather presenter, the organisers thought it would be a good idea to keep her standing on stage while I performed, because that's where she'd stood during all the corporate speeches. Don't get me wrong: I have nothing against weather presenters. But you don't see me hovering over their shoulder while they do the four-day-forecast.

But I digress. Considerably. The corporate gig I was booked to do after the 2005 Comedy Festival was for a bunch of finance workers employed by the public health sector. In a nutshell, accountants. People not generally renowned for their sense of humour. So it was with some trepidation that I approached this corporate gig. But it was being held at a resort on the Great Ocean Road and they were putting me up for the night. So I thought 'Bah – I'll do it, it'll be fine.'

I turned up to the resort and no sooner had I walked in than I noticed a really nice-looking guy standing at the bar. But he was talking to a pretty girl who I assumed was his partner and besides that, I was there was for work, not play. So I did the gig, which ended up being okay; the audience were pissed but at least they were upright. After the gig finished the woman who'd booked me took me aside and said, 'Look, this might be out of line but I saw the show you did about being single and I've been listening to you on the radio for a while now, so I sort of feel like I know you. There's someone here I'd like to introduce you to that I think you might like.'

Now at this point I have to point out that I'm generally a pessimist. Some people see the glass half-full; I see it half-empty and chipped. And, as you probably remember from your single days, when someone tries to matchmake you, you usually get introduced to someone you probably wouldn't piss on even if they were on fire. Seriously. One of my cousins tried to matchmake me once. She introduced me to a guy I certainly wouldn't have pissed on, but after he'd had a few too many drinks later that night, he let me in on his little secret – occasionally, with the right person, he liked to be the one doing the pissing.

Hearing this guy say that raised a number of questions for me, like: when exactly does wee become sexy? At what point does 'Ooh, I need a wee' become '*Ooh, I need a wee.*' When have you been in a bar, seen someone attractive and found yourself thinking 'Gee,

I wouldn't mind pissing on them?' Who do you define as 'the right person'? Someone absorbent? And what part of a guy who likes pissing on people did my cousin think I would like?

So you can imagine my surprise when the woman at the gig introduced me to the nice-looking guy I'd noticed when I first got there. The Bloke. Someone I *would* piss on if he was on fire. The two of us hit it off that night and now we're married, which makes The Bloke the longest one-night stand I've ever had.

The Bloke and I have often wondered whether our paths would have crossed if he hadn't been at that conference or I hadn't been booked to do that gig and I don't think they ever would have. So I guess corporate gigs aren't all bad, although I do believe it's well and truly time The Bloke stopped introducing me to people as 'the entertainment'.

THE BLOKE

Throughout this book you will find many references to The Bloke. The Bloke is my husband and the reason I refer to him as 'The Bloke' is because the only condition he has ever put on me talking or writing about him is that I can only do so if I let him stay anonymous. And that's fine, but you probably need to know at least a little bit about him:

- His favourite word is 'ubiquitous' because he likes the way it sounds.
- Because he grew up in the country, he refers to going to the city as 'going into town'.
- Sometimes while watching SBS he reads out the subtitles in the accent of the country the movie comes from.
- I haven't heard him sing since the 3rd of October 2006 when I caught him singing the jingle to the Cadbury Chocolate commercial . . . while he was on the toilet.

- When he was a kid, he wanted to know what he'd look like with a black eye, so one day he got a friend to stand with their fist at his eye level, then he ran into it at full pelt. He says he looked good.
- He once pondered aloud whether Valentine's Day was a busy day for hookers.
- He harbours an intense dislike of Elmo because he thinks Elmo killed Grover's career.
- He cannot for the life of him understand why they recently made a movie about Beatrix Potter. When told it's because she's a well-loved author, he replied 'So's Max Walker. And nobody's making a movie about him.'
- He hates Leunig cartoons. In 2007 we had a Leunig calendar on the back of our toilet door. One day I walked past the toilet while The Bloke was in there for the long haul and heard him angrily muttering: 'Festival Of Alans this in the mouth, you shit-box. Take that, toilet-bowl. Blame it on Leunig. And don't act like you don't like it.' That's a quote.
- One of his favourite pastimes is throwing bartenders off guard by ordering cocktails that don't actually exist. Last week he ordered a strawberry daiquiri and a 'punch in the undies'.
- When I told him I'd just read a news article that said feminists make better wives, he immediately replied 'So do Romanian gymnasts'.
- Once, when I asked him what he was thinking about immediately after sex, he answered, 'windchimes'.
- He once turned down the radio in the car so that I could 'really appreciate the sound of this fart'.

He's quite the catch.

The Bloke in his natural habitat

fINDIng 'The one'

People often talk about how you know you've found the person you're meant to be with. When I was single I remember married people telling me things like, 'When you find that person, you'll just know', which I always thought was something that married people just said to reassure themselves that they'd made the right choice.

Personally, I always preferred the theory of the philosopher Plato (because I'm a complete wanker). Plato had a theory about perfect love, and it involved the idea that as human beings, we are all born as halves of one being and in order to become whole again we need to find our other half.

In light of what I've learned after all my time with The Bloke, I agree with both those explanations but I also think that love can also come down to a matter of practicality. I'm a pretty straightforward person – I decided The Bloke was the one when I got out of the shower one night and saw that he'd put my PJs over the heater so they'd be nice and warm for me. At least I think that's why he did it – either that or he was hoping they'd catch fire and I'd have to sit on the couch to watch *Star Wars* with him in the nude.

I asked The Bloke when he started thinking I might be the one and he reckons it was when I cleaned up after his dog. The Bloke owns the world's biggest beagle. His name is Eddie, although Eddie's not fussy – he'll answer to everything from his own name to Mr Poopie.

World's biggest beagle – extreme close-up

The Bloke honestly reckons he knew I was the one when I cleaned up Eddie's poo. The Bloke came in from the backyard one Saturday morning and said, 'I think Eddie's constipated. I just went out to clean up after him and there was nothing there.' After telling him that was because I'd already been out there with the poop-a-scoop, The Bloke immediately got the same look on his face that you'd expect someone to have if you'd just said, 'By the way, I've paid off your mortgage and Oprah's given you a car.'

Then he just stood there for a while until he finally said, 'No-one's ever done that for me before.' And I thought, 'You know what? I should hope not.' How odd if every now and then, someone just knocked on your door and asked if you had any poo that needed collecting. Although come to think of it, it might make Jehovah's Witnesses more popular . . .

The main thing I learned from all this was that if you want a guy to fall in love in with you, you have to be prepared to get your hands dirty. And if you want a girl to fall in love with you, you have to put her PJs over the heater in winter. Putting her undies in the freezer in summer doesn't really have the same effect.

How The Bloke Proposed

Before I was actually proposed to I didn't really know much about wedding proposals. I mean, I knew the basics: I knew a wedding proposal should be romantic, I knew it should be a surprise, and I knew that, ideally, the person being proposed to should know a proposal when they see one.

When The Bloke proposed it was romantic but it was also such a surprise that I had no idea what was happening even while it was happening.

On the 23rd of March 2007, The Bloke and I went to dinner at our favourite restaurant. Then, at The Bloke's suggestion, we went for a drive to a scenic lookout with a cool view of the city skyline. It was there that The Bloke insisted we get out of the car – in the rain – to get a better look at the view.

At this point I had no idea what was going on, which I've since learned makes me a bit of a dick. Because I know women who would have cottoned on before they'd even seen a menu at the restaurant.

One of my friends reckons she knew her partner was going to propose 'because of the way he did his hair that night'. What? With a big spiky bit in the centre that he could hang a ring off? Another girl told me – and I personally think this is bullshit – but she swears she knew her partner was going to propose 'because of the look on his face when he woke up that morning'. What? Like a strangled fart? But my favourite way of knowing came from one of my sister's friends who reckons she knew her partner was going to propose 'because he wore deodorant'. And good on him for making a special effort. In many ways that was obviously one of the best days of his girlfriend's life.

I, on the other hand, stood in the rain with absolutely no idea and yes, it does get worse. The Bloke took my hand (still no idea) looked into my eyes (still no idea) then he sank down to the ground on bended knee.

My response to the guy who, unbeknownst to me, was quite clearly preparing to propose? 'Don't do that, you'll get your pants dirty.'

Dickhead. Dick. Head.

It wasn't until the occupants of a panel van, which had pulled up to the lookout just in time to catch the show, started honking their horn excitedly at us that I figured out what was going on. First I said sorry, and then I said yes.

So that was the proposal. And yes, I still cringe when I think about my first reaction. And The Bloke's not in any hurry to let me forget the whole don't-get-your-pants-dirty thing: not long ago he sent me an email that contained no text. There was no message. Just twenty-four pictures that he'd downloaded of people with dirty pants.

THE RING

The thing I liked most about The Bloke's proposal was that it didn't involve a ring when it happened – although I found out the reason for that later on. I've always been a bit suss on ring-based proposals. No offence if you were proposed to with a ring but it's always struck me as a bit of a bribe. You know, 'Marry me and I'll give you this!'

But for some women it's all about the ring and it becomes a bit of a status thing. There are women out there who think the bigger the diamond, the more important they are. Which is ridiculous. I've never seen anyone on a packed tram give up their seat to someone who was wearing a bigger diamond. I've never seen anyone take 23 items through the 12-items-or-less queue and get away with it by saying 'Sorry everyone, bigger diamond'.

There's too much emphasis on the ring and it makes me feel bad for the guys doing the proposing. One day while I was having coffee with one of my sisters she took a call on her mobile from her best mate, Mark, who was planning to propose to his girlfriend, Cassie. He was in a jewellery shop, trying to decide on the ring, and their conversation went like this:

Mark: 'I've narrowed it down to two rings. One of them is the style I know Cassie would really like but the other one's really big.'
My sister: 'That's easy – get the style you know she likes.'
Mark: 'But I thought bigger was better when it comes to diamonds?'
My sister: 'That's not diamonds, Mark, that's penises.'

Poor Mark. He'd grown up hearing everything from 'diamonds are a girl's best friend' in the movies to 'size doesn't matter' in the bedroom and in one fell swoop my sister shattered everything.

The reason The Bloke's proposal didn't involve a ring turned out to be quite simple. The day after it all happened we were talking about it and I said, 'So, were you nervous in the lead-up to the question?' and he went, 'Nup.' Then I said, 'But you'd planned the dinner and the lookout and the knee thing?' and he went, 'Nup.' When I asked him what he meant he replied, 'I didn't specifically plan to ask you last night. We got about halfway through dinner and I just thought . . . fuck it.' Now, on the one hand, that's mildly offensive. But on the other hand at least I know I wasn't being bribed.

So while there was no ring in the proposal it was the first thing most people asked about when I told them I was engaged. Everywhere I went it was, 'Show us your ring! Show us your ring!' which I wasn't really expecting. So after I'd spent about a week responding to those requests by pulling my pants down and bending over, The Bloke decided that maybe it was time we went jewellery shopping.

Now I don't know what people usually do when they go engagement ring shopping because I'd never done it before. And I wasn't one of those women who knew exactly what sort of ring she wanted because she'd been fantasising about it from the age of fourteen. And those women are out there.

I sat next to a girl in Year 8 who had cut-out magazine pictures of diamond rings stuck into a page of her school diary. I remember asking why and getting the answer, 'So that when the time comes, I'm ready.' That's kind of weird. I mean, you buy condoms so that when the time comes, you're ready. Although for all I know that's what she'd stuck onto the next diary page. Ooh, look: there's frangers in February.

So that was her. I, on the other hand, had no idea about diamond rings because I had pictures of

New Kids On The Block in my school diary. But because I had no idea, The Bloke suggested we go out and try a few styles to see what I liked. Which kind of made ring shopping sound like the Kama Sutra. I had visions of trying on rings with my ankles round my ears.

So off we went jewellery shopping and it was here that The Bloke had a brainwave: why try on rings in an expensive jewellery shop in the city that's filled with snooty sales assistants? If you're just trying on styles to see what you like, why not just go to a shopping mall?

So we did. But we didn't just go to any jewellery shop at a shopping mall. We went to one called Chic As. You know they're not expensive because they can't even afford the rest of the sentence. Chic As what? I think you need to know the rest of the sentence because the rest could make all the difference. You might think it's 'Chic As Audrey Hepburn In *Breakfast At Tiffany's*' when it may, in fact, be 'Chic As Britney Spears Getting Out Of A Car And Flashing Her Flange'. There's a big difference.

Turns out this place was 'Chic As Long As You Don't Want A Real Diamond'. It's a jewellery shop where everything's made of cubic zirconias so you get the look of a diamond without the price. It's the jewellery shop equivalent of Dannii Minogue.

The sales assistant we had was named Shaz. Which I loved, because it fully entitles to her use the phrase, 'I'm Shaz from Chic As'. And Shaz was great. When we told her we just wanted to try a few different rings to see what we liked and then get a jeweller to make the real thing, she said, 'Why bother? No-one's gonna be able to tell. You could buy a stone from here that's as big as your eyeball and tell people it's real and they'll believe you.' When I asked her why I'd want a stone that big, Shaz replied, 'It might get you a seat on the tram.'

Long story short: we found a style, had it made and when I put it on for the first time I thought, 'Well, I never thought I'd see the day, but the receipt for this thing says no exchange or refund so I guess I'm getting married.'

WhAT YouR RIng SAYs AbouT YoU . . .

You've heard of navel-gazing. This is all about contemplating your ring. As in, the one on your finger. Come on – you know it never stops being funny.

I'm buggered if I know why, but some women get competitive when it comes to their ring. These are the women who only look at your ring long enough to provide a segue into talking about theirs. These women are generally superficial and very good at backhanded compliments. For example, 'That's pretty. I didn't know they made jewellery that nice at Goldmark.'

Remember the following descriptions so that if you ever fall into conversation with one of these women, you can feign interest in their ring long enough to dish them one of the following lines (starting with 'I read somewhere that your type of cut means . . .).

Round cut: Your friends all got one like this and, being conformist, you got one too.

Princess cut: You're high-maintenance and demanding but, on the upside, this is probably the first big purchase Daddy didn't make for you.

Emerald cut: You're not into girly things, preferring gardening and dirt bikes. Are you sure you're not a lesbian?

Marquis cut: You're an attention-seeker with self-esteem issues. I'll bet you saw this cut in a movie once. Was it something with Barbra Streisand?

Pear cut: You're perennially constipated and need as much fruit as you can get.

Oval cut: You tend to be difficult and just wanted to guarantee the diamond-cutter had a real shit of a day.

PART

Two

Be prepared . . .

bRIDAl EXPo

Here's the thing: I never planned on getting married. I'm not into frills and I hate wearing dresses so I certainly never wanted to be a bride. I've never been afraid of the commitment side of things – I always planned on sticking with The Bloke but we'd never really talked about actually getting married. I think we pretty much just planned to hang out together until one of us died. So as much as The Bloke's proposal came about because he thought 'Fuck it, I'll ask,' my saying yes came about because I thought, 'Well, fuck it, I'll accept.'

But from the moment that happened I went from a lifetime of being anti-bride to suddenly being bride-curious. Which is kind of like being bi-curious, but the websites are nowhere near as interesting.

Being bride-curious meant that suddenly, I was a little bit interested in weddings. Which is why one of the first things I did after being proposed to was go to a bridal expo. But I didn't really go for tips and ideas about wedding planning. No, I went for the same reason anyone ever goes to an expo: I went to get me some free shit.

And I nearly did – literally. Because the first thing I saw on display at the expo were portable toilets, which made me think, 'Looks like wedding planning's a load of crap.'

I dragged The Bloke along with me but he clearly had no idea what to expect from a bridal expo because the first thing he said when we arrived was, 'Do you think we'll see any fights today?' I clearly recall turning to him with hands on my hips, saying, 'Why would there be any fights here? What kind of white-trash place do you think this is?' Then we went inside . . .

. . . where we found people fighting each other over cupcakes. I kid you not. There were a couple of wedding cake companies who were promoting themselves by handing out samples and, of course, there weren't enough to go round. But there were some women there who were going in hard: I actually heard someone use the phrase 'That bitch just took my cupcake'. It was like they'd confused cupcakes with donor kidneys. These were quite clearly women who'd been on pre-wedding diets for just that little bit too long.

Unfortunately, cupcakes were pretty much the only freebies there: everyone else was just giving out fliers and discount vouchers. Every time I turned around someone shoved another piece of paper in my face to the point where I just started taking stuff without even looking at what I was taking. Which is why I didn't notice until I was about to leave that somewhere along the line someone had given me a flyer for plastic surgery.

Yeah, because the first thing you should do after someone proposes to love you forever just the way you are is change everything. That's a great idea. According to the flyer, my wedding checklist should include normal things like buying a dress and booking a photographer but I should also set aside time to reshape my nose, suck the fat out of my arse and get a new set of breasts. Because apparently, nothing says 'I do' like brand new boozies. Although it would give a whole new meaning to the vow of 'to have and to hold'.

Interestingly, the flyer didn't mention anything about male plastic surgery. Which is a shame, because what could make a wedding night more memorable than a surprise penis extension? Preferably on the groom. But the flyer did offer a special deal whereby if the bride booked in for plastic surgery, the bridesmaids and mother of the bride would all get 20% off their plastic surgery as well. Which I love. Because that's pretty much saying, 'Not only are you not attractive enough to get married but your mum and your bridesmaids are ugly as well!'

The plastic surgery flyer really pissed me off although I did feel better after I flushed it down a portaloo. But I wasn't the only one who'd been mildly disturbed by the expo. When I asked The Bloke why he didn't want to talk to any of the caterers at the expo, he replied, 'Do *you* want to talk to a man with a ponytail?' He then refused to watch the fashion parade on the grounds that everything at the expo had already given him 'sore eyes'.

It was at that point that I knew he was over it so I left him to have a beer at the café while I went to look at the honeymoon displays. And I'm giving the award for dodgiest-sounding destination to a place in Fiji called – and I'm not making this up – Vomo Island. If it's pronounced 'Voh-moh' it's probably fine. But if it's pronounced 'Vommo' I think I've been there a few times before but I can't say I've ever enjoyed myself.

So I went back to the café but The Bloke wasn't there. And I panicked, thinking, 'I've broken him.' But as it turned out he'd been off getting right into the swing of the expo thing because a few minutes later he came back shouting, 'Come over here – I've found a guy who was voted best Victorian wedding photographer three years in a row . . . and he's giving out free chocolates!'

Should I Attend a Bridal Expo?

It depends on how easily you panic. I went to two bridal expos: the first one was at the very beginning of the planning process and the second one was about halfway through. The first one made me feel stressed out about all the things that needed to be organised but by the time I attended the second one, I'd realised that you don't actually need to have and do half the things that bridal expos and magazines say you do, so I was able to enjoy the expo more and use it to get ideas and information about the stuff I was genuinely interested in.

A really important thing to bear in mind about wedding expos is that first and foremost, they're money-spinners. If you let a bridal expo dictate everything you had to have for your wedding, you'd be looking down the barrel of half a million bucks in expenses. So I suggest you don't go to a bridal expo thinking you have to have everything that's on show.

Bridal expos are, however, brilliant for giving you the opportunity to speak to a range of industry professionals all under one roof. Florists, cake designers, transport companies, even dance instructors are all there to show their skills (and price lists) and answer any of your questions.

And you'll certainly get ideas and inspiration from an expo. Sometimes those ideas will be for what not to do – The Bloke and I took one look at the stretch

Hummers on display and promptly decided they were the tackiest form of transport we'd ever seen in our lives. Other times those ideas will be brilliant. For example, The Bloke and I found a company called Wedding Co and used their services to set up a free personal wedding website. We printed the web address on our invitations and the site allowed our guests to access information about our wedding that wouldn't fit on the invite, such as travel and accommodation listings. I hadn't seen this company advertised anywhere else and if we hadn't found them at the expo we wouldn't have set up our website.

So by all means attend an expo if you're after some ideas but stay calm, don't let anyone talk you into plastic surgery and don't be afraid to bitch-slap someone for a free cupcake if you have to.

BLOKE'S WORLD

Bridal expo

Let's face it: you don't know everything there is to know about organising a wedding and the only way you're going to read bridal magazines is if they start including nude centrefolds. So going to a bridal expo with your Nearly-Wife is a great starting point for getting your head around some of the products and services you might like to have as part of your wedding.

The disadvantages of going to an expo are that you'll have to give up an afternoon and, at some point, your Nearly-Wife will probably have some form of panic attack. The advantages of going are that there'll be heaps of cars on display and the fashion parade will definitely include a lingerie section. I think you'll find the advantages speak for themselves.

SETTING THE DATE

Attending my first bridal expo not long after The Bloke popped the question made me realise that, apparently, we had to set a date for the wedding. (I know – who'd have thunk it?) The question I kept getting asked at the expo was, 'So. Have you got a date?' Which initially inspired me to respond the same way I responded when people asked me to show them my ring, but nobody likes to flog a joke.

The Bloke and I hadn't discussed a wedding date and I didn't think there was any rush to set one . . . until I spoke to my dad.

My dad, George, is a wonderful dad. He's also an accountant, which explains why his favourite joke is, 'What did the constipated accountant do? He worked it out with a pencil.' Dad's skills as a joke wizard are thankfully surpassed by his skills as an accountant, and the latter were well and truly on display when The Bloke and I rang him to say we were engaged. Dad's response? 'Congratulations . . . I'll get the calculator.' Immediately.

Dad also had a firm view on setting a wedding date and he laid it all out like this: 'You'd better not waste too much time if you want to start cranking out kids.'

This response came as a bit of a shock to me because it's not like I'm staring down the barrel of menopause. For God's sake, I'd only just turned thirty – which is a sentence I'm sure I'll be repeating for at least the next fifteen years.

But Dad's comment played on my mind a bit and, at one point, I started thinking maybe I *should* have a baby and try to get pregnant specifically for the wedding – stuff the boob jobs on offer at the expo, think of what pregnancy does for your cleavage! That was all sounding great until The Bloke pointed out that if I was pregnant at the wedding I wouldn't be able to drink. Which pretty much turned 'Let's get pregnant!' into 'Forget it'. Because, as far as I'm concerned, if a bride can't drink her weight in champagne before slagging off a few relatives, starting a conga line on the dance floor then passing out face-down in her own wedding cake, the terrorists have already won.

In the end, The Bloke set the wedding date: 25th of May 2008, which was exactly three years to the day after we met. Romantic, right? I know. But before you vomit into your shirt sleeve, here's why he chose that date: not because of its significance, simply because it's 'one less date to remember'. He's not romantic. He's retarded.

Choosing Your Date (nudge, wink)

I know you don't need me to tell you when to get married but here are just a few things to bear in mind when picking a date. Ha! It never gets old.

1. The warmer months are usually the most popular because of the good weather (really?) so if you want to get married during this time book early because venues fill up fast.
2. While the warmer months are the most popular, the cooler months are cheaper. Seriously. Many venues offer 'non-peak' wedding rates during May, June, July and August to keep their businesses going and if you're looking to keep your costs to a minimum, this is a terrific way to start.
3. Similarly, weekday weddings are also cheaper and depending on the venue, Sundays can be too. A Friday afternoon wedding is a great way to kick off a weekend of wedding celebrations and provided you give them enough notice so they can make arrangements with their employers, your guests will

probably love having a legitimate reason to avoid working on a Friday afternoon.

4. This is quite possibly the girliest thing you'll ever hear but if you have your heart set on using a particular flower in your bouquet or floral arrangements, check when it's in season before you set your wedding date. It's not impossible for florists to source flowers when they're out of season (they can often source them from up north or down south, depending on what you're after) but they will charge you an arm and a leg. Literally. When I asked my florist about the possibility of having gardenias in late May, she quoted me the entire left-hand side of my body. Which I probably should have taken her up on, because I would have saved money on my dress if I'd only needed half of it. Don't question my logic, okay?

5. If you're having a destination wedding, choose a date that takes full advantage of that destination. For example, if your wedding's at a winery you'll want to make sure your date coincides with when the vines are lush and full as opposed to dormant and bare. Note also that sometimes dates can also help you choose your destination: friends of mine who wanted to marry in winter because that's when they met actually had their wedding at an Alpine lodge in the Victorian high country during snow season and it was breathtaking. Bloody freezing, but

breathtaking. They even had snow domes as their wedding favours. Very cute.

6. Make sure the date you choose doesn't clash with a friend or family member's important celebration. You don't want to choose a date, book a church and venue and then realise the date clashes with your cousin's Bar Mitzvah. Or whatever.

BLOKE'S WORLD

Setting the date

If you're a footy nut, don't set the date for grand final day. I know you've seen movies where people at weddings listen to the game through an earpiece but odds are that won't cut it in real life.

Similarly, if you play competitive sport don't set the date for your finals season. That's assuming you're good and a chance. If you're shit, book away, wooden-spooner!

Whatever date you choose to marry, commit it to your memory for the rest of your life. No woman ever withheld sex because her husband marked their wedding anniversary with a beautiful bouquet of flowers and the words, 'Best day of my life.' Go get 'em, tiger!

THE BUDGET

I have to let you in on something that you'd never know unless I told you: as I typed the words 'The Budget', I burst out laughing. I'll tell you why.

The Bloke and I didn't have a budget for our wedding. Not because we're fabulously rich, just because we had no idea how much wedding things would cost so we had no idea what to budget for them. We just made sure we got a few quotes for everything as we went along (except the cake, which we fell in love with instantly) and went with the people and prices we liked the most.

So we never had a budget to start with but even if we had, we wouldn't know whether or not we went over it. You see, despite the fact that we have all our wedding receipts and invoices in a little file marked 'wedding' we've never actually added everything up.

We just can't bring ourselves to do it. The fact is that we both feel like our wedding and honeymoon were the most brilliant times of our life together so far and we don't want to run the risk of ruining how we feel about them by doing the maths and figuring out *WE SPENT HOW MUCH?!* So we'll never know. You've heard of sticking your head in the sand – we're sticking our head in the confetti.

So the idea of me writing a chapter to give you advice on your wedding budget makes me laugh out loud. Essentially, I can't do it. Every bit of advice in this book is borne of my own experiences planning my wedding but seeing as I didn't draw up a budget for myself, I can't very well tell you how to do one, can I?

You'll find some detailed money-saving tips throughout the chapters of this book but here are some general tips that might come in handy when you're thinking about your wedding and your hip-pocket:

- Keep your drink of choice handy. No, really.
- Decide what you think is a reasonable price to pay for things as you go along. For example, as The Bloke and I got quotes for things and thus gained more of an understanding of how much things cost, we tried to set limits on how much we wanted to spend on flowers, photos, wedding favours, etc. I found this easier than coming up with one overall

number for the total costs involved in a wedding and then trying to stick to that.

- Offer your parents and Almost In-Laws the opportunity to help with costs, and note there's a big difference between offering and demanding. Consulting with parents is best done in the early stages of planning so everyone knows where they stand from the get-go. And try to do some early numbers because they'll probably want to ask you some specific questions about how much they're up for. For example, my parents and The Bloke's parents were keen to cover the cost of our reception but they had a few questions about how many people we were planning to invite and what the average per-head charges are these days.

- Always shop around. It takes time but it's absolutely, positively, one hundred per cent worth it when you're trying to get the best possible price.

- Be open-minded and prepared to compromise when it comes to costs. Some things will end up being cheaper than you thought they'd be but a lot will end up being far more expensive.

- Don't be afraid to negotiate with wedding service providers – it's worth it.

- The fewer guests you have, the less your wedding will cost.

- Keep your invitations simple. Simple invitations will cost less than la-di-da ones.

- Getting married off-peak will save you money. The cooler months are great months for saving, with many wedding service providers (especially venues) charging less to entice business.
- A Saturday wedding will cost you more than a wedding on any other day of the week.
- One-stop weddings (same location for ceremony and reception) will save you site fees.
- Wedding lunches are cheaper than wedding dinners.
- Use your wedding cake as your dessert and pay for a two- instead of a three-course meal.
- Providing the alcohol for the wedding yourself can often be cheaper – do the numbers and compare.
- A DJ will be cheaper than a band.
- Consider a non-bridal bridal gown. Bridal gowns aren't the only white dresses and how cool would it be to be able to get more than one wear out of your wedding dress?
- Choose flowers that are in season.
- Consider renting rather than buying where you can. This is especially handy for things like suits and other outfits, and even decorations.
- If you know someone who sews, bakes amazing cakes, DJs, arranges flowers or has any other skills you could use for your wedding, talk to them about your needs for your day.

I read somewhere recently that the average Australian wedding costs around $28,000, but I'm sure you could do it cheaper. I'm also sure you could spend way more than that – it all depends on your choices and your financial situation. There's no point putting yourself into massive debt for the sake of one day, albeit an important one. By the same token, some things are worth spending money on. The point of the day is not to show off how much cash you've dropped and neither is it to skimp on adequately lining your guests' stomachs. The point is for you and your Almost-Husband to celebrate your love for each other with all your family and friends.

Now, let's all have a drink!

THE GUEST LIST

When it came to drawing up the guest list for our wedding, The Bloke and I had a problem, that problem being that The Bloke wanted a small wedding. That's not actually a problem in itself until you consider the fact that my family background is Greek.

Greeks don't know what a small wedding is. My parents think they had a small wedding. In fact, they'll look you in the eye when they tell you that their wedding was 'tiny'. My parents had 220 guests. And unfortunately, their way of thinking is in my DNA.

I wanted to invite *everybody* to our wedding. Family, friends, pets, you name it. I'd be willing to bet that if you and I had met and bonded before I'd sent wedding invitations out, I would probably have wanted you and your Almost-Husband on my list.

As much as I would have loved to have a small nation attend, the reality is that weddings are expensive – more so than they were in our parents' day – and having large numbers makes your costs skyrocket.

The simple fact is that you can't invite *everybody* but some people ark up if you leave them out. The Bloke and I made things even more difficult because we did that thing where you invite everyone to the engagement party to try to cover all your bases there so you can try to just have close friends and family to the wedding. But that gets really awkward because when people are saying goodbye to you at your engagement party, they say things like, 'See you at the wedding!' while you're standing there thinking, 'Uh – no, you won't. And I am such a bitch right now.'

Our wedding venue could fit up to 200 people but, in the interests of keeping tables to a manageable size and not crowding the room, The Bloke and I agreed on 130, which meant we had to cull the never-ending list I'd come up with. One night The Bloke and I were going through all the names and there was a group of people he suggested we should cut. I was mortified and told him we couldn't possibly cut them because even though we hadn't seen each other for a long time, I'd grown up with them. To which he responded, 'Well, you also grew up with Humphrey B. Bear but we're not inviting him.' Harsh but fair.

DRAWING UP YOUR GUEST LIST

This part of the planning process can often get a bit hairy, but take a deep breath and you'll get through it. Obviously, your final guest list will be determined largely by the capacity of your reception venue. Once you know what your venue limit is, start by making a list of all the people you'd like to invite and have your Almost-Husband do the same. Then set aside some time and a bottle of something perky and go through your lists together.

Firstly, consider the family members on your lists. Decide who your absolute must-haves are and put them on an 'A' list. Put all other family members on a 'B' list for the moment, then repeat this exercise with your friends. And yes, I know the idea of putting anyone on a 'B' list sounds harsh but doing this makes it easier if the number of people you think you might like to invite exceeds your venue's capacity.

Add up all the people on your 'A' lists and if the final number doesn't exceed your venue's capacity, you're clear to start assessing who you can invite from your 'B' list. (Note: you'll be safe if you did a rough guest list before you locked in your venue, as we'll discuss in the venue chapter.) Assessing your 'B' list is where things can sometimes get tricky, but there are some basic questions you can ask yourselves to help make your selections easier. Is the person you're considering someone you see often? Are you likely to continue to see them often after the wedding? For example, if it's a workmate and you're thinking of changing jobs soon, there might be someone else on your 'B' list that you'd be better off inviting.

Are you thinking of inviting someone to your wedding simply because they invited you to theirs? This particular issue is a massive ballbreaker, let me tell you. There are still a lot of people who think inviting you to their wedding is a guarantee they'll get invited to yours but I'd argue that's not always a strong enough reason to invite them. If their wedding was five years ago and you've only seen them a handful of times since then, consider carefully because you might be inviting them at the cost of not inviting someone you see more often.

Workmates can be tricky customers, too. There's no rule that says you absolutely have to invite them, for starters. If you are going to invite them, invite only the workmates with whom you have the best relationship. If your boss is an arsehole, you don't have to have them at your wedding. Similarly, inviting one workmate from sales doesn't mean you have to invite the whole team. Be discerning and consider, objectively, your relationships with these people. If you think inviting some workmates and not others will create a total shitfight at the office, you might have to reconsider having them there or be prepared to face a possible backlash (see People Have Cracked It, page 47).

As far as inviting partners goes, there's no rule that says you have to invite people you've never met (i.e. the wife of someone you're inviting from work) and doing so can blow out your numbers and budget. Similarly, the days of nonchalantly slapping the words 'and partner' on the invitation of a single person are all but gone. And note that they're also potentially risky: I recently heard a great story about a 'plus one' that – unbeknownst to the invited guest – turned out to be an arch-enemy from the groom's past. He fumed, I laughed my arse off and there's a lesson there for all of us.

Despite that, there can be exceptions. For example, allowing a guest who's not part of your main family or friendship group to bring a partner or friend often means they'll enjoy themselves more. The Bloke and I gave one of our guests the option to 'bring a friend' because apart from us, she didn't know anyone else at the wedding. Ultimately it's up to you to use your judgment according to your venue capacity, budget, and how you feel about the prospect of people you've possibly never met being at your wedding.

Your parents might also want to have some of their friends at your wedding and they might also want a say in which family members you invite. Here's where this part of the process can get the hairiest in terms of trying to keep everybody happy. If your parents are footing the bill for the entire day it's probably fair enough that they have some people of their choosing attend, but try to find a happy medium. Their friends shouldn't outnumber yours and if they want to invite someone you really can't stand, speak up before old touchy-feely Neville tries to give you a once-over on the day. The 'Parents' chapter will give you some ideas and support regarding parental issues and contains a totally boss letter you can use if they're still sending you round the bend.

PEOPLE HAVE CRACKED IT THAT THEY'RE NOT ON THE GUEST LIST – HOW DO I HANDLE THIS?

Most people understand that weddings are personal affairs and that in this day and age, they're becoming more and more expensive, so hopefully you won't have too many people taking you to task. However, for every understanding person there's a high-maintenance dickhead. No, really. I think that's actually a proverb.

If you're faced with someone who has the balls to suggest you should be inviting them to your wedding, try to placate them by explaining your numbers are limited by your venue or budget but you'd love for them to be part of the day by attending the ceremony. Or, if you're having pre-dinner drinks before your reception and your venue is amenable to it, you may wish to include them in that. If they still kick up a stink, there's every chance that they are in fact a dickhead and who wants dickheads at their wedding anyway?

Should we Invite children To oUR wedding?

Depends. Can you save money on service staff by getting them to walk around with trays of hors d'oeuvres on their heads? Do the children actually belong to other guests or are you just picking kids off the street? Are they likely to bring you a gift that's not fingerpainted? Just kidding.

Some people are anti-kids at their wedding because they don't like the idea of them running amok at a formal occasion, which kids are known to do. Kids don't care if it's a formal occasion – once they hear there'll be dancing and cake, they're as good as climbing the walls already. Other people don't mind kids being at their wedding as long as the parents are happy to keep them in check, and other people don't care either way.

Personally, I like the idea of kids at weddings. I think it's auspicious to have them attend and I also have great memories of going to weddings when I was a kid. I remember thinking they were like fairytales come to life and feeling very grown-up and special to be there. The Bloke and I made all our guests who were parents aware that kids were welcome at our wedding. Some of them brought their little ones and some of them didn't, and the ones who didn't chose that option because they wanted to let their hair down without being reported to Child Services.

If you'd like to invite children either put their names on their parents' invitation or do what The Bloke and I did and write 'Children welcome – just let us know with your RSVP'. Make sure that your venue can provide children's meals and if the kids are old enough to sit in a 'big chair', allow for them in your table arrangements. If they're still in highchairs, check whether your venue provides them (many do), and notify the parents if they don't. If the kids are still in prams, you might like to consider seating the parents at a table on the edge of the room rather than smack-bang in the middle so their prams aren't in the way and they can manoeuvre them in and out of the room without causing a commotion. And if you're God's gift to children and it's within your budget, you might even like to provide a colouring book and pencils, a puzzle or a game to any kids who are old enough for them – it will keep them amused during speeches and they'll love you for it. Just don't provide any toys that are noisy, unless of course you want the video of your wedding speech punctuated by the sound of Hungry, Hungry Hippos.

If you don't wish to invite children, leave their names off the invitation. If any parents don't get the hint and ask if they can bring their kids, there are two basic options. You can give them the 'limited by venue and budget' line or you can just explain that you'd prefer your wedding to remain adults-only due to the formality of the occasion. If you have a guest who's a breastfeeding mother you might like to make an exception if it's the deal-breaker between her being able to attend or not, with the added benefit that she'll be handy to have around if the kitchen runs out of milk when it's time to serve coffee.

BLOKE'S WORLD

The guest list

Don't invite any ex-girlfriends. Trust me on this. Alcohol often does strange things to people and the ex you thought was cool with you getting married might just turn into the raving drunk who grabs the microphone and starts singing 'What About Me' halfway through the speeches.

Inviting everyone in your footy or cricket competition will not go down well, I promise. Take them out for a drink instead. Odds are they'll actually end up shouting *you* and you can avoid the very real chance that Macca will bail your new bride up at some point during the reception and break the cardinal rule of 'What happens on the end-of-season trip stays on the end-of-season trip' during conversation.

And please note that when considering the people on your 'B' list, large breasts should not be a deciding factor in getting anyone over the line (female or male).

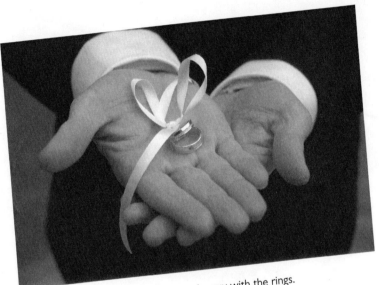

And don't forget to invite the guy with the rings.

THE INVITATIONS

When it came to our invitations, The Bloke and I were adamant that we didn't want anything that looked too fussy, formal or girly. What we did want was something unique and personal that was both a reflection of us as well as of the kind of 'look' we wanted for our wedding. I was also really keen to use the invitation as a starting point for a theme we could continue through the rest of our wedding stationery: place cards, menu covers, order of service booklets, our kitchen fund gift registry card, RSVP cards, wedding favour tags and later, our thank you cards (I'm a Virgo – I like everything to match).

We'd seen heaps of examples of wedding invitations and wedding stationery designs at the bridal expo and nothing really grabbed us. Too much pink, too many hearts and flowers and way too many swirly fonts.

Either that or it was all too modern and funky for our tastes, so we decided to design our own invitations and have them printed up. One of my sisters has a friend who's a graphic designer so we knew she'd be able to produce whatever we came up with and we also knew that she'd be cheaper than a stationery company. Mate's rates are indeed a wonderful thing.

As soon as The Bloke and I agreed we really liked the idea of using a photo on our invitations, there was one that immediately stood out as being perfect. About a year after we met we went on holiday to Glenelg, South Australia. Our hotel room had a little balcony that overlooked the ocean and one evening we started taking photos as the sun went down. The Bloke set up the camera so it was elevated and then set it to 'auto' so we could have a photo of the two of us together. In the time it took for a pash and a camera flash we ended up with a photo of the two of us against a backdrop of the most awesome, richly-coloured sunset.

There are three things I really like about the photo. First: we're in complete silhouette – you can't see our features but you can tell it's us. Second: because you can't see our features you can't tell we're both pissed. Seriously – the first thing I did after we took the photo was try to go inside by walking through the screen door. And the third thing I like is that it's the most perfectly composed photo but it was all a complete, champagne-fuelled fluke.

If you drink then pose you're a bloody idiot.

TIPS FOR YOUR INVITATIONS

1. Regardless of whether you design your own invitations, have a professional do them for you or buy them ready-made, consider theming your wedding stationery because it really does make a terrific impact and people notice. Theming doesn't have to involve the same image repeated over and over: colours, fonts and even textures can be used to tie all your stationery together and make the look more personalised.

2. Allow your invitations to provide your guests with their first taste of what your wedding will be like. If it's a high-class, formal affair, go with a similar look on your invitation: maybe a Hollywood-style art deco font, feathered background and black velvet ribbon. If you're planning a relaxed beach wedding you could use a photo of your wedding date written in the sand and use clear glue to attach a sprinkle of real sand on your invitation. Doing your invitations is a fun part of the planning process because you can be as creative as you like.

3. Using a photo of you and your Almost-Husband is the perfect way to make your invitation a one-of-a-kind (especially if you use actual police mug shots). One of the best invitations I've ever seen was a postcard the couple had made showing a series of four shots they'd taken of themselves in a photo booth. In each photo they held a sign, so what you read was 'Finally . . . we're . . . getting . . . married!' The design plus the fact that they were pissing themselves laughing in the photos gave the invitations a really happy look. It wasn't just a great idea, it was also an accurate reflection of the couple and the casual, fun wedding they had planned.

4. If you're having your invitations done professionally, shop around and compare prices. And offering to order all your wedding stationery from the same company at the same time is also a good

bargaining tool as you can often get a better price on a bulk order.

How Do I word MY InvITATIoNS?

In short, any way you friggin' like (although you might like to avoid the use of the word 'friggin' on your invitation). Once upon a time wedding etiquette dictated that invitations had to be worded quite formally. The invitation was usually issued by the bride's parents, along the lines of 'Mr & Mrs Whoever request the pleasure of the company of the guest to the wedding of their daughter to some guy at such and such a time and place' (well, not exactly like that but you get the drift). There were also different formal wordings for different situations, such as when the invitation was issued by the groom's parents, the bride and groom's parents together, the bride or groom's divorced parents, the bride or groom's widowed parent, the bride or groom's widowed but remarried parent – and the list goes on. Very traditional wordings tend to get more and more complicated as the issuing parties do. And while there's certainly nothing wrong with following tradition (and many people still do), there are also less formal and – you guessed it – more personalised options for you to choose from.

For example, rather than attempt to run the gamut of options when it comes to issuing an invitation from your parents or your Almost-Husband's parents – whatever their marital status – you can start with a phrase like 'Together with our families . . .' Or you can omit the mention of family altogether and issue the invitation from yourselves (although you might want to run that by your folks if they're footing the bill for the whole shebang).

The initial wording of your invitation can be as simple or as eloquent as you like. The best example of a simple one that I've ever seen just said 'Tom and Ellie are getting married', and then listed the wedding details. On the eloquent side, I have seen invitations where the couple have composed poems or used famous quotes, or chosen simple opening phrases such as 'We invite you to share the beginning of our adventure of a lifetime'. That one kind of made me wonder whether the couple was getting married or whether they'd been accepted as contestants on *The Amazing Race* but it was cute, it suited them and it conveyed how they felt about getting married.

When composing the wording for our invitations The Bloke and I looked at the hundreds of examples you can easily find on the net for inspiration. Then we came up with this:

Together with their families
TERRI and THE BLOKE
are ridiculously excited to invite
YOU
to celebrate their love and marriage

And all the official details came after that. We liked that this wording began with the word 'together' and we knew the 'ridiculously excited' line would make our guests smile as well as reflect how we felt (until we started getting the bills for everything).

What Information Should I Include on My Invitations?

As far as official details go, your wedding invitation should include the following essential information:

- Wedding date.
- Location for the ceremony/reception.
- Times for the ceremony/reception.
- RSVP details.

When it comes to RSVP details make sure you include the RSVP date, which is usually no later than three weeks before the wedding. You should also specify who you'd like your guests to RSVP to (will it be to you or to your parents?) and how you'd like them to RSVP (by phone, email or in writing?).

For our wedding, The Bloke and I included stamped, self-addressed RSVP postcards for the guests to mail back to us. The postcards showed the sunset photo from our invitation on one side and the other side had space for our guests to write their names and tick a box to say whether or not they were attending. There was also a spot for them to say whether they were bringing any kids and another few lines for them to write down any special food requirements, such as whether they were vegetarian or coeliac.

While the fact that our RSVP postcards were stamped by us meant that we doubled our postage costs (one stamp for the invitation, one stamp for the postcard), we thought this would be the easiest way for our guests to promptly respond with all the required information. What we didn't expect was the handful of guests who instead chose to RSVP by phone because they wanted to keep the postcard stuck on the fridge as a memento!

Other information you may wish to include on your wedding invitations, depending on whether you think it's appropriate, could be:

- Relevant map details.
- Dress code.
- Parking information.

Gift registry information shouldn't go on your invitation but should instead be enclosed with it. This used to be considered presumptuous but most people seem to do it now. Your gift registry provider should give you a bunch of little cards with all your gift registry information so you can put them in the envelope with the invitation.

If you want to provide your guests with accommodation or transport information, this can also be enclosed with your invitation. The idea is to keep your actual invitation to the basic information and provide other details separately – this keeps your invitations simple and uncluttered and enables you to have a clearer layout. If you don't like the idea of packing so much information into one envelope, you might like to do what The Bloke and I did and set up a wedding website to list all the extra information and just put the link to the website on your invitation instead.

When Should I Send My Invitations Out?

Wedding invitations should be sent out at least six weeks before your wedding. If your guests need to make special travel or accommodation arrangements I'd send them out sooner – we sent ours out a full two months before because we had guests coming from interstate. If you're getting married overseas or if attending your wedding will involve any other considerable expense, the more notice you give your guests, the more likely they will be able to attend. Many people send out 'save the date' cards for this reason – they're not a full invitation but merely a little card that contains the date and location of the wedding to enable guests to make the necessary arrangements. If you're sending these out, ensure you write 'formal invitation to follow' and then make sure you actually invite all the people you've told to save the date. No point asking old Aunty Sue to keep Saturday, 5th of February free for your wedding if you're not actually going to invite her to it (God knows she'd rather be wearing a shiny tracksuit down at her local RSL while spending your inheritance on the pokies).

Ensure you have someone proofread all your wedding stationery before you order or print it. Don't assume someone at the stationery company will do it for you. And if you're doing your own invitations, don't rely on any spellcheck functions because they won't pick up incorrect grammar.

How Do I Manage RSVPs?

The Bloke is mad for spreadsheets (blame his professional finance background) so he put together an Excel document with all our guest information on it. The document showed the guest list, a complete list of addresses, who was coming, who had special food requirements, who was bringing kids and whether the kids would require kids' meals/chairs, and then another column for thank you cards for us to use after the wedding. I have to hand it to The Bloke because he pretty much managed all the RSVP information himself – mainly due to the fact that I knew nothing about Excel. And I loved having one less task to organise.

The advantage of managing RSVP information this way is that you can collate everything in one document and if you set it up properly, the program will make all the calculations for you regarding guest numbers, special meal tallies, etc. You can even program it so you get a running tally of your costs depending on how many guests reply with a 'yes'. This beats a big handwritten folder of information that can be cumbersome and God help you if you lose it. The other advantage of having everything on computer is that you can back it up and if you save everything onto a data stick you can even take it to work with you and do wedding stuff there, all the while looking as though you're busily going about your job. No telltale wedding folders to give the game away? Perfect.

BLOKE'S WORLD

Invitations

Don't want your invitations covered in hearts and flowers? Get involved, my friend! Regardless of whether you and your Nearly-Wife are having your invitations and stationery done professionally or you're designing them yourselves, you should totally have a say. And you'll want to, considering the fact that invitations are usually the starting point for setting the tone of your day as far as things like theme, style and colours are concerned. You'll be kicking yourself when the seven shades of pink on the invitations you played no part in coming up with start appearing everywhere else throughout your wedding day.

If you're an ideas man, throw your hat into the ring when it comes to helping create a concept or look for your invitations and stationery. Do you have an eye for photography or a bit of artistic skill? Get cracking. And if you're a dab hand at graphic design or layouts there are opportunities ahoy for you to be hands-on here. The Bloke played a big role in the design of our wedding stationery and got a real kick out of fielding compliments on it and saying, with feigned modesty, 'I designed that myself.'

If you're not the creative type but you have a head for figures, put yourself in charge of the RSVP list. Put together a spreadsheet and update it as the RSVPs start rolling in. Then make it your job to phone any guests who haven't replied by the RSVP date. This is a pretty straightforward but no less important task that your Nearly-Wife will appreciate you taking on. She's already got enough to keep track of – trust me.

THE DRESS

You might not know this but there'll actually be three major players in your wedding: you, the guy you're marrying and your dress. Regardless of how you feel about dressing up or being the centre of attention (trust me – not everyone's into it) there's no denying that your wedding dress is an integral part of the day. Your walk down the aisle will be a hotly anticipated, unforgettable moment from the perspective of your Almost-Husband and all your guests. And, like it or not, people will be dying to see what you're wearing – hopefully not literally (although that could be handy if you need to cull your guest list but aren't sure how).

I'm not really a girly-girl but I'll tell you this for free: your dress is really important. Even if you're like me and you have no interest in fashion (seriously – if I ever even imply that I care about what they're wearing on the catwalks of Milan, you have my happy permission to punch me in the clam).

There'll be many opportunities for you and your Almost-Husband to express yourselves throughout your wedding, but your dress is just for you. It's an expression of your style and personality but it can also be a bit like the foundation of the whole day: the look and the feeling created by your dress is something that actually goes beyond you. I don't want to get too cheesy on your arse but whatever mood you want to create for your big day – party, formal, romantic, casual, old-fashioned – it all starts with your dress.

I put off shopping for my dress for as long as I possibly could because I thought I'd hate the entire process and would have trouble finding something that didn't make me look and feel foofy.

While I was right about not really enjoying the process (which could have had something to do with the fact that I hate clothes shopping at the best of times), I somehow managed to end up with a dress that I not only loved myself sick in but that also appeared to have super powers: not only did it do wonders for hiding my lady-lumps but it also seemed to have a magical effect on children.

I got ready from my parents' place, where my flower girl, Siena, and one of our pageboys, Marcus, were also getting ready. From the moment these kids saw my dress they immediately went from extremely excited to serenely glazed. All of a sudden buckles were fastened, hair was combed and ribbons were tied without fuss. At the reception our other pageboy, Will, was similarly entranced. Usually delightfully chatty and boisterous, Will kept coming over to wherever I was just so he could quietly sit by me and trace the sparkles embroidered into my bodice. That dress was kiddie-Valium!

Even though I didn't really enjoy the process of looking for a dress I was amazed by how much I learned. The first thing I learned was how important language is when it comes to bridal wear. Apparently it's not a *dress*, it's a *gown*. I've only ever worn a gown when I went to hospital for my wisdom teeth, so I can't say I was into the idea of going to my wedding wearing something made of paper that had my arse hanging out of it. (Although I still can't figure out why they needed access to my arse when they were pulling out my teeth – I would have thought my mouth was the obvious entry point for that one but hey, I'm not a doctor.)

According to one bridal-shop attendant, the reason your outfit is referred to as a wedding *gown* is because it's 'more than just a dress'. Yeah, it's more. About four thousand dollars more. And if the gown is couture? Couture, for those of you who don't know, is French for 'fucking expensive'. And bridal couture means 'You want this gown? You sell your car'.

The second thing I learned is that all bridal-shop attendants speak in hushed tones. Bridal shops are kind of like libraries. Walk into any bridal shop anywhere and I guarantee the attendants will whisper to you. Although I don't know why, because unless they're selling wedding gowns out the front and burying people out the back, there's no reason for them to talk like that.

The third thing I learned was that trying on a wedding gown isn't as easy as you'd think. When I was in the fitting room, trying to put the gown on by putting it over my head, the bridal-shop attendant laughed at me. Apparently you're not meant to put it on over your head, apparently you're meant to 'just step into it'. Like it's a dog poo. A very, very expensive dog poo.

But I know what you're thinking: how did the shop attendant know I was trying the gown on the wrong way? Because she was with me in the cubicle while I was practically nude. This is the fourth thing I learned: one of the first things the shop attendants do is look at you in your bra and undies to get an idea of your exact body shape. At least, that's what they say. It doesn't explain the photos on the net and the footage on YouTube.

One bridal-shop attendant spent so long staring and whispering at me while I was in the semi-nude that for a while I thought maybe she was trying to get me to put out. Turns out she wasn't, which was disappointing because I'd kind of hoped it might get me a discount on the gown.

Some of these attendants were nuts. One of them told me I should seriously consider the benefits of padding my breasts. Now at first that was all right because I thought she said 'patting'. And yes, there are benefits to that – it feels nice. Although I don't know why you'd do it while you're walking down the aisle. But then I realised she'd said padding, whereupon I was tempted to suggest she should seriously consider the benefits of padding her head because that might make it less painful when I punched her.

But my favourite experience by far was with the guy I ended up buying my gown from. His name is Shane, I'll refer to his shop as the House of Shane and while he wasn't actually in the fitting room with me while I was trying things on, we did bond. Seriously, you haven't lived 'til you've had a man you've only just met tuck your back-fat into a bodice.

TIPs To hELP YoU RocK YoUR fRocK

I know sweet, sweet nothing about wedding dresses. Where do I start?
Buy a bunch of bridal fashion magazines and cut out pictures of what you like the look of. Bear in mind that

what you like the look of might not necessarily end up being what looks best on you but you'll sort that out when it comes to trying things on.

Cutting out pictures of dresses from magazines might make you feel eight years old again but it's a great starting point. (Note: I also advise consulting page 291 while you go through these magazines to dull the pain that occurs once you see the cost of anything bridal.)

The first great thing about this exercise is that once you've been through a few magazines you'll start to notice common threads – excuse the pun – between the pictures you've cut out. It may be that you've got a penchant for a certain dress style or feature that you didn't even know you had: a certain neckline might keep appearing, you might see similarities in the sort of skirt shapes you're leaning towards or a certain type of embroidery detail might keep popping up.

The second great thing about this exercise is that it will enable you to start articulating exactly what it is you like and what you don't. Good bridal magazines won't just feature a photograph, they'll also have some information to go along with it. This will allow you to go from turning up to a bridal-wear shop and asking to try on 'a dress where the back is sort of long but not and then goes into a kind of circle' to turning up and asking to try on 'a dress with a puddle train'.

Similarly, knowing some of the lingo means that when a dressmaker suggests that she make your bodice rouched, you'll be familiar with what the hell that means and able to say whether or not that's what you want. When it comes to bridal wear, getting your head around the lingo does wonders when you've no idea where to start. Think of how much easier it would be to take your car to the mechanic if you were able to articulate precisely what the problem was and understand exactly what your mechanic was crapping on about when he rang to tell you what he was going to do about it.

The third great thing about cutting out magazine pictures is that if you're working with a dressmaker or bridal-shop attendant who has had a good look at you and gained a clear understanding of your body shape, it can save you heaps of time. When I showed my portfolio of favourite pictures to my designer Shane, he immediately put three of them to one side. The reason? 'These are all tapered skirts and they'll make your hips look twice their size.' Fantastic. In less than thirty seconds he saved me the pain of trying on tapered skirt after tapered skirt and wondering why it didn't look quite right. The less you have to try on dresses full of hope and then take them off full of confusion and/or self-loathing, the better.

Do I buy off-the-rack or should I have my dress made?
This depends on a few things. If you're pressed for time (shotgun wedding, anyone?), you should definitely buy

off-the-rack. You can still get a dressmaker to make any minor adjustments but you'll have your dress much quicker than if it was being made from scratch.

The size of your budget can also determine whether or not you have your dress made. Generally speaking, buying off-the-rack is cheaper. Having your dress made by a dressmaker involves paying for your pattern, your fabric and the dressmaker's time and labour. Similarly, a bridal couture designer who designs something just for you will factor in the cost of their design, the fabric, and their time and labour, too.

However, if time is not an issue and your dress is fairly simple in terms of design and fabric, a dressmaker can sometimes be cheaper. This is where your portfolio of favourite pictures comes in handy: take it to a couple of dressmakers and ask them to give you a rough quote.

I'm having my dress made. When do I start?
Now! Just kidding, but if you're having your dress made I'd advise that you get cracking at least 8 to 10 weeks before your wedding. And you're going to need a pattern or design, fabric and a dressmaker.

As far as finding a dressmaker goes, personal recommendations are priceless and far more desirable than just picking someone out of the Yellow Pages. If you don't have a recommendation and you're going to let your fingers do the walking:

1. May the Lord be your Shepherd, and
2. Make sure you start by visiting a few different people so you can look through their portfolios and chat to them about exactly what you want, how much it will cost and the timeframe you're looking at for turnaround. You can also take this opportunity to talk to them about bridesmaids and flower-girl outfits if you're having these made too.

Unless you're a dressmaking expert I would strongly advise against buying your fabric before you've secured your dressmaker. Imagine buying metres and metres of top-dollar, top-quality silk only to be told by a dressmaker that the fabric doesn't suit your style of dress. While I'm not suggesting you let a dressmaker dictate your fabric purchase completely, it's certainly wise to check with them before making the big spend to make sure you're buying the right material in the right amounts.

In terms of patterns, again: try before you buy. Try on the style you're thinking of in a bridal-wear shop, make sure it's what you want and then buy the pattern. Don't buy a pattern on sight only, have it made, try it on then have some sort of nervous breakdown when it's not what you wanted or what suits you.

I'm buying off the rack. Where do I start?
Internet bridal porn. I'm serious. Google 'wedding dresses' in your state and start visiting the websites

of stores and/or designers with retail outlets. These websites will give you an idea of the places you should visit to start trying stuff on and the places you should avoid like cholera, unless you want to look like human fairy floss. In addition to your magazine pictures, these websites will help shape your ideas about the kind of dress you want and most will give you some idea of price.

I received great advice about where to start shopping from my already-married girlfriends. If you liked the look of someone else's dress, don't be afraid to ask them where it came from and if you're feeling brave – or drunk – find out exactly how much it cost.

While we're on the subject of cost – I could sit here and tell you how important it is to have a budget and stick to it but that would make me a big fat hypocrite. The fact is, I had no idea how much a wedding dress cost when I started looking because, like you, I'd never done this before and I had no idea what I was up for.

I pulled the figure of $3000 for a dress out of my arse (not literally – I don't want you thinking I was trying out some sort of anal Tattslotto) but that went out the window when I visited the House of Shane and fell in love with my couture dress, to the tune of $4800.

I'm not ashamed to tell you I then haggled along the lines of pay-less-pay-cash and I'm also not ashamed to tell you I then went without waxing and many other personal expenditures in the lead-up to the wedding in order to afford that dress. (The going-without-waxing thing actually worked out quite well because it enabled everything – and I mean EVERYTHING – to grow out completely so that my pre-wedding wax was the best, most thorough wax I've ever had. Although if you ask The Bloke about my going-without-waxing thing, he will simply grimace and make a joke about *Gorillas In The Mist*.)

My point, however, is that once I fell in love with that gorgeous but over-my-budget dress, nothing else compared. I visited store after store in the hope that I'd find something just as nice but cheaper, but nothing even came close. So my sage advice to you is this: if you have a budget of any kind, don't even tempt yourself by visiting a couture designer because it will only result in tears and/or the hairiest legs you've ever seen. And if you're not sure about a bridal-wear shop because their website doesn't have a price list, there's no shame in calling to enquire before you visit in order to ensure you don't fall hopelessly in love with something you can't afford.

But, I hear you ask, was your dress worth going over your budget for? You're not going to want to hear this, but yes. I can't tell you how much I loved every inch of that gown. But I also would have loved having a bit more cash to splash around on facials, massages, manicures and oh, I dunno – petrol – in the lead-up to the wedding. And I'm pretty sure I could have shouted

The Bloke a few extra pre-wedding treats, too. In any case, if all goes to plan I'll make that cash back with the Baby Bonus. Like the way I rationalise?

Who do I take dress-shopping with me?
In the early stages of looking for your dress, I advise taking one or two Brutally Honest people only. Once you've narrowed your dress choice down a little bit you can take other people along if you want to. You don't have to take four bridesmaids just because you've got four bridesmaids – they're not your posse and you're not in a bridal-themed episode of *Entourage*.

One or two Brutally Honests will give you one or two perspectives you can trust. Three bridesmaids plus your mum plus two shop attendants could potentially give you six wildly different opinions and a possible brain aneurism. Consider yourself warned.

I had three bridesmaids for my wedding – my two sisters and The Bloke's sister – and in the early stages of dress-shopping I just took my sisters. Once I'd narrowed my dress choice down to a few I started bringing my mum along, which she and I made jokes about at the time because Mum's vision-impaired. Because of this I made sure that all the appointments we attended were in the morning when there would be plenty of natural light and I also ensured that the shop attendants we dealt with understood we would probably need extra time.

While she couldn't see the detail in everything I was trying on as well as everyone else could, Mum had great gown advice and it was important to me that she was part of the process. And that's something worth bearing in mind: even if you don't think you need your mum's opinion or worse, if she's a faffer when it comes to shopping and you don't want her faffing while you're trying to make important decisions, try to bring her along at some stage (even if it's just to show her what you've chosen). Mums love that shit. Besides, mums have usually already swanned around in a wedding gown so they might just have some good advice for you about yours.

When I'd narrowed my dress choices down to two, I also brought my dad to help me make the final decision. Not only does Dad have a good eye but – and yes, deep down I'm a big softie – I wanted both him and my mum to be there when I made my final choice.

Mum and Dad knew I had a preferred dress out of the two but they didn't know which one. The fact that both of them chose my favourite sealed the deal. Dad's an accountant and when I told him how much the dress cost I expected a lecture. Instead, he simply almost fell over. Then he said, 'How many times are you planning on getting married?' When I answered, 'Just once,' he said – and I quote – 'Then bugger it. Buy the dress.' Mind you, when my next tax return came around he also sat me down and gave me a half-hour lecture that included the words 'sensible', 'budget' and 'imperative'. I also recall the phrase 'living within one's means' being bandied about so don't worry – he eventually made his point!

What do we do when we get there?
Regardless of whether you're visiting a bridal-wear shop or a designer's retail outlet, always make an appointment and always be on time. Appointments aren't always compulsory in all stores but I recommend making one to save you from driving all the way across town only to find the place chock-full of noisy slags commandeering all the gowns and the attention of the assistants with nothing left over for you. There. I've said it.

When you arrive, show your designer or shop assistant any pictures of what you like and try to articulate the look you're going for. If you don't like ultra-modern styles or you really want something that looks like a party frock, say so. Giving your designer or shop assistant as much information as you can up-front helps them to help you.

Similarly, don't be shy about letting them get a good look at you. You might feel embarrassed (I definitely regretted not waxing), but having your designer or shop assistant know your body shape from the outset makes it much easier for them to recommend the most flattering styles.

In the early stages of your browsing, try on as much as you can – even gowns (and colours) that don't initially grab you. There are two reasons for this: something that doesn't appear to be much chop on the hanger might look fabulous on you, and something you never thought would suit you might actually look hot.

Trying on dress after dress can be overwhelming – after a while everything starts to look the same. After the first day of appointments I felt like my brain had turned into ricotta cheese, so I started spreading my appointments out over a couple of weeks instead of trying to cram them all into a couple of days. This was better because it didn't overload my brain capacity. It was also better because my sisters and I topped off each day of appointments with a cocktail, and why would you only get two cocktails when you could stretch it out to five, I ask you?

Most places don't allow any photography in order to guard against people ripping off the designs, so when you try on something you like have one of your Brutally Honests note down the following: which shop you're in, a brief description of the dress including the style and the fabric, and a design number if you can find one. And if that sounds like a bit of a silly thing to do, re-read the first sentence in the previous paragraph. Having this information handy will make life much easier when you re-visit places as you narrow down your dress choices. Nobody wants to try on 47 dresses twice.

What should I be looking for and thinking about while I'm trying on gowns?
Old hypocrite-lady here suggests keeping your budget in mind for starters. Other than that, try to avoid focusing on one particular part of your body and aim to assess what each dress does for your shape overall. Initially, I was so fixated on my thighs that it took me ages (and a rather pointed suggestion from a designer) to start looking at what a dress could do for my overall figure. Once I mastered this skill I started referring to it as The Force and trust me: when you learn to use The Force, shopping for your wedding gown becomes much less traumatic.

Paying attention to what different styles do for your shape will enable you to start narrowing down what sort of design is best for you. The main areas to look at are:

- The cut and shape of the skirt. Be sure to assess this from all angles, as a skirt that looks great from the front might make you look like the back of a truck from the rear.
- The cut and shape of the neckline. Pay particular attention to whether it makes you look broader or narrower across the shoulders and whether or not it balances out your hips.

- The backline of the dress. If it has a low back, should the shape of the backline taper to suit yours or would a wider scoop be more flattering?
- The sleeves. Is a sleeveless, strapless or capped-sleeve style best for you?
- The colour and type of fabric. Does white or ivory suit your skin tone? What fabric suits you – and the style you're seeking – best?

Initially, all this might sound confusing but you'll start to work out what you like and what works best on you with each dress you try on. Just don't fall into the trap of buying a dress under the assumption that you're going to lose ten kilos. Trust me. You won't. A little bit of weight loss you can probably aim for if you're going to diet and/or exercise but don't buy a size ten if you're a size fourteen.

Some people will tell you that you'll lose weight due to 'stress' but again, that's entirely negotiable. What if you eat more when you're stressed? I'm not really a stress-eater and despite the fact that I exercised more before the wedding, I somehow managed to put on weight for my final fittings, so go figure.

If you're having your dress made, a dressmaker will also allow for weight fluctuations either way . . . unless they're a complete mole. Upon attending her final fitting one of my friends was alarmed to discover her dress was quite tight. When she mentioned this, her dressmaker replied, 'I thought you'd lose more weight than you have.' Last-minute alterations plus a few days of living on soup and my friend's dress fit her perfectly, but I still maintain that her dressmaker was a mole and in need of a good bitch slap.

As you begin to narrow your style choices down, the final and most important factor to consider is what I call the 'user-friendliness' of the dress. How easy is it to wear? How comfortably will you be able to walk/sit/dance/bend/breathe? Will you be in constant fear of your norgs popping out? If the skirt has a long train, will you have to lug it around all day or can it be pinned up?

I was very particular when it came to the user-friendliness of my dress. I wanted it to hold, mould and streamline my waist, hips and tummy but I also wanted to be able to move about freely and – most importantly – I wanted to be able to dance without it looking like I was doing The Robot. My dress had a very structured bodice which held everything in place and had the added benefit of straightening my posture but the skirt was the opposite: it was made of really light liquid satin. It was so fluid it felt almost weightless on, and the train was long (for the ceremony) but had a little hook-and-eye that enabled it to be bustled up into the rest of the skirt (for the reception).

That dress was the ultimate in user-friendliness . . . until the hook-and-eye broke during the bridal waltz and the train unfurled. Amazingly, this occurred at a point in the dance where it looked like it was actually meant to happen. It also occurred at a point in the night when I'd had enough drinks that I didn't care. Besides, you haven't lived until you've seen a bride dance Zorba The Greek into the wee hours with her couture skirt hoiked up over her shoulder.

Final points to remember:

- Don't be afraid to take your time when making dress decisions. If you feel like a shop assistant is rushing you into a purchase you're still unsure about, ask her if there's somewhere else she needs to be.
- Don't let yourself be bullied by a designer. If you're having your dress made specifically for you, make sure you're getting exactly what you want. Especially if you're paying couture prices.
- Trying on dress after dress will seem overwhelming at first but narrowing down your choices based on your likes and dislikes will happen naturally until you find 'the one'. That's how you found your Almost-Husband, right?

BLOKE'S WORLD

Suit Yourself

When it comes to wedding wear for blokes, I know exactly what you're thinking. And to answer your question: yes, you DO have to wear a suit.*

How did I know that's what you were thinking? Because that's the first question The Bloke hit me with when we started talking about his wedding outfit.

In fact, our conversation went like this:

THE BLOKE: 'Do I *have* to wear a suit?'
ME: 'A suit? No, stuff that. Wear your jeans and your Johnny Cash T-shirt. No, go on – you'll look great.'

And that's all I said. And we left it.
Then the next day he kicked off again:
THE BLOKE: 'So do I have to wear a suit?'
ME: 'A suit? No, stuff it. Wear the boardshorts you got in Sydney. You know, the ones you put a hole in when you were fixing the shed and now, sometimes, from certain angles, a little bit of your nut hangs out? Bugger the suit, wear those.'

And that's all I said. And we left it.

---

* The only way you wouldn't have to wear a suit would be if you had a beach wedding in which your bride wore a white bikini and you wore budgie-smugglers.

The next day I told The Bloke that I was making him an appointment for a male Brazilian so that when his nuts popped of his boardies, at least they'd look tidy.

And that's all I said.

And we left it.

And the next day, he went out and bought a suit.

Well, technically, he hired one. I tried and tried to talk The Bloke into buying his suit outright for two reasons:

1. If he spent money on his suit it would make me feel better about the sweet, sweet cash I was throwing down on my dress, and
2. If he bought a suit it meant that he would have one to see him through formal functions for the next ten or twelve years (or if he followed the example set by my dad, the next thirty). In the end The Bloke decided to hire his suit because he wanted a three-quarter length jacket which he didn't think he'd have cause to wear again in the near future unless, in his words, 'I cark it on our honeymoon.' Mmm, yes. Pragmatic *and* positive.

Regardless of whether you rent or purchase, the most important factor in choosing your suit is to know the look you're going for. Are you going for a modern, traditional or vintage look? To a certain extent this will depend on the look your Nearly-Wife is going for, and while you've probably got about as much chance of plucking out your own pubes as you have of getting your Nearly-Wife to describe her wedding dress to you, if you can at least determine whether her look will be modern, traditional or vintage you'll be able to ensure that your suit complements her dress.

When it comes to suits, shirts and ties for you and your groomsmen, it might be worth getting a bit of fabric from your Nearly-Wife's dress and the bridesmaids' dresses so you can make sure your colours tone in. I'm serious. What's the point in buying expensive ties if it turns out they clash with the colour of the bridesmaids' outfits? And how impressed is your Nearly-Wife going to be when you ask her for a fabric swatch? (That's the technical term for a sample bit of fabric. Watch your Nearly-Wife's eyes pop out of her head when you casually drop it into conversation.)

The right colours are important because not only do you want to look good on the day but you don't want to look back on your wedding photos and think, 'That shirt looked really shit.' Consider whether you want to wear a pure white or an off-white shirt. If your Nearly-Wife is wearing ivory, off-white on you lessens the chance of her dress looking 'dirty-white' in comparison.

The Bloke got off lightly when it came to colours because he's actually colour-blind. It's true: he's got no idea his jocks are blue, he's oblivious to the fact that my eyes are hazel and he's an absolute bugger to play against in a game of Guess Who, because when I ask something like 'Does your person have brown hair?' he'll reply, 'Buggered if I know. Will I win if I say yes?'

In terms of the colour of your suit, blacks, browns and greys are okay. Reds, greens, yellows and any other colours you think will be 'hilarious' will not. I can guarantee that your Nearly-Wife will not appreciate hilarity when it comes to your wedding day attire. Save that for your wedding night. (I highly recommend those elephant undies where your wang becomes the trunk. Okay, whatever. Forget I said anything.)

When it comes to you and your groomsmen sorting out who pays for what, the general rule nowadays seems to be that groomsmen pay for their suit and the groom pays for everything else – shoes, ties, shirts, cufflinks, etc. However, everybody's budget is different and it's worth discussing this with your groomsmen in the early days of your planning. Even if you're purchasing your suit you might like to think about having your groomsmen hire theirs – a good suit is a big investment that not everybody can afford. If you really want them to buy their suits so that they match yours, you might consider going halvies. Regardless of how you end up splitting the costs with your crew, you should at least make sure you shout their cufflinks or ties as a thank-you for having them stand up for you at your wedding.

Finally, be aware that nobody – and I mean nobody – cares how much you loved Marvin the Martian: novelty ties at weddings are out. And ditto novelty sleeves. Personally, I've never really understood novelty sleeves. Why bother with a shirt that makes you look normal when you've got your jacket on but then turns you into a champion knob the minute you take it off?

THE FAFFING

According to most bridal magazines, you're expected to spend six months and a small fortune on faffing around to get yourself match-fit for your wedding. We're talking a regimen of weight loss, cellulite elimination, hair treatments, nail care, foot care, moisturising, exfoliation, micro-dermabrasion, plucking, waxing and tanning, all scheduled in regular appointments and carried out with military-like precision.

You know what I reckon? Bugger that.

Unless you've got a face like a smacked arse, nobody needs that much work. Repeat: nobody. Six months of all those beauty treatments? You know who you'll end up looking like? Michael Jackson. The irony being that he *does* have a face like a smacked arse.

And weddings are expensive enough without adding six months' worth of costly beauty treatments.

The idea that you have to blow all this cash on all this crap is just another example of the money-spinning that's part of the wedding industry. The beauty treatment side of the industry identifies and cashes in on every bride-to-be's insecurities about not looking her best on her wedding day. By all means treat yourself before the wedding, but let's be realistic and sensible here. Here's how:

YOUR WEIGHT

If you're planning on going from a size 14 to an 8 in six months, think again. It's impossible to lose that much weight safely within that timeframe and if you starve yourself or embark on some crazy diet whereby you only eat lemons/brown foods/cotton balls, chances are you'll feel like crap and look much the same.

The whole idea that brides-to-be should slim down gives me the shits anyway, so I say: instead of aiming to get skinny, aim to get healthy. This will do more for your appearance than anything else because every inch of you will benefit. A healthy, well-balanced diet coupled with sensible exercise will not only do good things for your waistline but your skin will glow, the condition of your hair and nails will improve and you'll feel terrific as well.

You know the drill: aim to eat three well-balanced

meals with lots of fruit and vegetables per day. Snack healthily but don't deny yourself your favourite treat occasionally. Drink lots of water, consider taking a multivitamin tablet and, if you don't already exercise or play sport, aim for 30 minutes of exercise per day to get your heart rate up.

As far as this media-driven obsession with ridding the world of cellulite goes, look at it this way: nobody's going to see it under your dress anyway. Google 'celebrities with cellulite' and cheer yourself up. Even so-called 'skinny' people get cellulite but if you're planning on a beach honeymoon and you're feeling apprehensive, let's get real about what you can do.

The fact is that nothing short of surgery or laser treatments will get rid of cellulite (hey – don't shoot the messenger). Expensive salon treatments that claim to make cellulite disappear won't, and ditto for over-the-counter products. The best that these products and treatments can do is improve the appearance of your skin but you can probably achieve the same results by eating healthily, drinking lots of water and using a good-quality body brush on your problem areas to increase circulation. (Some people claim that dry-brushing the skin gets good results but take care to be gentle so you don't cause irritation or damage – mitts with plastic or rubber nodules are often better for dry-brushing.) If using a cellulite cream makes you feel better, knock yourself out. Although, personally, I think you'd have just as much chance of beating cellulite by sprinkling your thighs with oregano while Gregorian chanting.

YOUR HAIR

The magazines will tell you that you need to start booking in for regular salon treatments now. You don't. If you want to have a special salon treatment such as a hydrating or conditioning treatment, have it done in the week before your wedding – these treatments don't achieve permanent results so why spend money on six when you only really need one? If your hair is super-duper dry consider purchasing a tube or pot of something that you can regularly use at home. Don't think it's going to work any better just because a gum-chewing 19-year-old with a bare midriff and too much eyeliner works it through your hair in a salon. Are your mum's/sister's/housemate's/ Almost-Husband's hands painted on?

If you have split ends, have your hair trimmed regularly to prevent the splits moving up the hair shaft and causing further damage. Keep your hairdresser informed of how you plan to wear your hair for your wedding to ensure the cut they give you will accommodate your style. Book your final cut and/or colour appointment before your wedding about a week before the big day – this will allow plenty of time for your hair to settle and ensure you have time to go back and change anything you don't like.

YOUR HANDS AND FEET

If you already have regular manicures and pedicures, I'm happy for you (and also mildly jealous). If you don't, six months of these treatments can prove very costly but there are ways around this. If you're wearing open-toed shoes and you want fabulous feet, book a pedicure in for a month or so before the wedding (to get your feet into shape) and another the day before the wedding (to spruce them up for the big day). Do some maintenance at home in between (such as using a pumice stone or foot scrub weekly and moisturising religiously) and provided you don't have hobbit feet, two pedicures is absolutely all you'll need.

Your hands will definitely be on display – people will want to look at your rings and your photographer may also get close-up shots of the ring exchange and the signing of the marriage certificate – so it's well worth paying them some attention. Even if you don't have long nails, you can still have beautiful hands. Again, having a manicure a month before the wedding and another the day before can work wonders towards making it look as though your hands have been professionally pampered all year, provided you do some at-home maintenance in between. The key to great-looking hands is keeping them hydrated. Keep a tube of hand cream in front of the telly and spend a little time moisturising your hands while you watch *Neighbours*. Massaging cream into the cuticles and nail bed will also encourage strong and healthy nail growth – when done consistently, this really works.

YOUR SKIN

When I was in high school, I was always one of those people who had okay skin most of the time but a face like a pizza whenever we had school photos. Every. Single. Year. So because I was a little apprehensive about what my face would have in store for me on my wedding day, I did spend a little cash and booked a course of four facials in the three months leading up to the big day. The facials used vitamin C-infused products designed to promote skin clarity and I thought they were great – again, no permanent miracle cures but my skin condition was good on the day. If you have facials or any other facial treatment such as microdermabrasion or anything else that makes my toes curl, make sure the treatment you have closest to your wedding day is no less than 5 to 7 days before – facials can sometime stimulate a little breakout and some treatments can cause redness and I doubt you'll want to be worrying about either the day before the wedding.

Because I'm so paranoid about it, I did faff around a bit when it came to my skin but I refused to go overboard in terms of what I spent. About the same time I started having the facials I invested in a pair of good quality loofah mitts, a moisturising shower gel and a big bottle of body lotion for dry skin. Once a week I did an all-over body scrub in the shower, really concentrating on calloused areas such as heels, knees and elbows, and areas prone to break-outs, such as my chest and back. And I also used the body lotion every single day. By the time my wedding rolled around, the dark patches of dry skin on my elbows had disappeared completely and the overall condition of my skin improved heaps – it was much clearer and softer. If your arms, décolletage and back are going to be on show in your wedding gown, it's well worth making sure your skin looks good as it will definitely be noticeable. Salon body treatments are lovely but they'll cost you a fortune – you can do the treatments yourself at home and if you use good quality products you'll get the same results.

YOUR HAIRY BITS

Let them grow! I'm serious. If you can put up with being a little hairier than usual and skip a couple of waxes in the lead-up to the one you have closest to the big day, you'll get the best wax ever – I promise. This is because after waxing, hair grows in stages: first there's the initial 'flush' of growth, which usually appears 3 to 6 weeks after you wax, depending on your rate of growth. There are also slower, often finer hairs that don't grow at the same rate and often appear within your 'but-I've-just-had-a-wax' timeframe. Skipping a couple of waxes enables your hair to grow through in full, which means you get a good, clean wax. And skipping a few waxes also means you can put the cash you're saving towards something else – mine paid for my facials. Whatever and however you choose to wax, don't do it the day before your wedding – aim for two or three days before to make sure any redness or irritation has well and truly gone.

To Tan or Not To Tan

Let's get one thing straight: looking like a carrot in a dress is not attractive unless you're marrying Bugs Bunny. I've seen so many brides look perfectly normal before their wedding but then somehow turn into an extra from *Star Trek* on the day. Why? Buggered if I know.

If you're getting married in summer, chances are you'll already have a bit of colour so an artificial tan probably isn't necessary. Winter weddings are a different story: I had a spray tan before my wedding because I was deathly pale and worried about how I'd look with a made-up face and pasty limbs, and I'm glad I did. My arms were so white they were practically fluoro. At least after my tan I looked alive.

Some things to think about if you are going to tan:

- Go the *lightest possible shade*. It will look weird if you're a completely different colour to your Almost-Husband. (Unless, of course, that's because you're from different racial backgrounds, in which case congratulations to both of you and my, don't I feel awkward . . . look over there!)
- Do not use tanning beds – they make you smell weird, can really dry your skin out and have been linked to skin cancer. (Note: those reasons aren't in order of importance.) Have a spray tan instead.
- Find somewhere that does spray tans with a green base – this results in a far more natural colour, is great for people with naturally pale skin and won't give you the orange look.
- Have your spray tan done no less than a couple of days before your wedding. It takes about 24 hours for the colour to fully develop and allowing an extra day means there'll be no tan-stains on your dress.

- Don't wax and tan on the same day – if you wax after you tan you'll remove the tan and if you tan on the same day that you wax it can often lead to skin irritation and a strange, freckled effect. Have your waxing done first and have your tan done at least 24 hours later, longer if your skin irritates easily after waxing.
- I repeat: the *lightest possible shade!*

SHOULD I HAVE A HAIR AND MAKE-UP TRIAL?

Definitely. It's worth spending a bit of money on this to guarantee there are no surprises (or tears) on your wedding day. Make an appointment for a trial as soon as you've chosen your hairdresser and/or make-up artist (recommendations and word-of-mouth are great starting points if you don't have anyone specific in mind; otherwise do an online search and look at photos of their work). Show them your dress (or a picture of it) so they can see the style they're going to be working with, and discuss your likes and dislikes when it comes to hair and make-up and the overall look you're trying to achieve. Photos or magazine pictures of looks you like can also be helpful and showing/explaining your veil is vital, especially to your hairdresser. If you're not wearing a veil but will have flowers or another headpiece, make sure you explain these too. A professional will use this information and their expertise to make a few suggestions and then continue to work with you until you're happy with where you're headed (so to speak).

My hair and make-up artist was someone I'd worked with before for TV gigs and she was terrific. I showed her my dress and explained I was trying to achieve an almost old-world, Art Deco look with subtle colours and shapes for make-up and hair. She had some books on art deco style and we flicked through them together, highlighting what I liked. Then I pretty much just sat in front of a mirror and watched the transformation begin.

At the end of your hair and make-up trial, you should look exactly the way you want to look on your wedding day (just without the dress). This will take time and some trial and error – if you don't like something, make sure you speak up and are clear about exactly what it is you do want. When you're all done, take some photos of yourself so they can be referred back to on the day of your wedding. You might also like to make note of the lipstick your make-up artist will be using on you so that you can buy some to keep in your Emergency Bag (see page 187) on your wedding day. And scheduling your hair and make-up trial on the day of another special function or just dinner with your Almost-Husband is a great way to get more bang from your buck because you'll have somewhere to go and show yourself off.

Whether you have your hair and make-up done at home or in a salon on the day of your wedding is really up to you, but personally I think having someone come to you is so much easier. If you're having everything done at your house (or wherever you're getting ready), liaise with your professionals about when the faffing should start and allow plenty of time. Ensure they have clear travel directions for where they need to be and make sure you provide them with a designated work area with a table or bench space, good (and preferably natural) light and easy access to powerpoints for their hair dryers and curling irons. And depending on how many people are being made up you may need more than one make-up artist or hairdresser. My hair and make-up artist did my face and the faces of my bridesmaids, flower girl and mum. She also did my hair but because it wasn't possible for her to do everything in the timeframe we had, she recommended another hairdresser to do everyone else's.

Bloke's world

The faffing

Think you're going to get off lightly in the faffing stakes? Think again. You're meant to look your best on your wedding day, too. Here's how:

- Got a double chin or bit of pud that you always hate the look of in photos? A little bit of healthy eating and exercise won't kill you but it will lead to photos you can look back on with pride. Six months out from the wedding, cut the crap from your diet and get moving for half an hour every day – it's what your Nearly-Wife will be doing so you might as well make it a team sport.

- As far as your hair goes, have a haircut a week before the wedding. Whether you go so far as to have a back, sack and crack wax is none of my business – personally, I've always thought the phrase sounds less like a treatment and more like the sounds ducks make.

- I know a guy who had a 'man-icure' before his wedding. Seriously. He's a mechanic and he didn't want dirty wedding hands. I understand completely if the idea of stepping into a salon is about as attractive to you as the idea of wearing a skirt and heels to the footy, but please spend some DIY-time on your hands. The day before your wedding, trim your nails and use a nail brush to scrub them free of any dirt. Why? There'll be photos of the ring exchange, the signing of the wedding certificate, the cutting of the cake, etc., and your hands will be noticed.

- You'll want your skin to look good in photos too. If you don't already cleanse and moisturise, consider making a start. And don't worry, nobody else has to know – it can be our little secret. You won't be wearing make-up on the day (unless there's something you're not telling me), so cleansing and moisturising regularly in the months leading up to the wedding will go a long way towards ensuring the skin on your face is in peak condition and free of blemishes. Similarly, if you're headed for a beachside honeymoon and you're self-concious, start using a back brush regularly in the shower to exfoliate the skin on your back and keep that blemish-free too.

- Unless your signature look involves stubble, psych yourself up for the mother of all shaves on your wedding day. Pay particular attention to the task so you a) look hot, and b) don't cut yourself to shreds. If you want to spoil yourself or you're just plain old-fashioned lazy, book yourself into a good barbershop for a professional shave — one of my mates swears by them for special occasions and reckons you really notice the difference on your skin.

Because you don't have nearly as much to do in the faffing department as your Nearly-Wife does, I'm going to throw something else at you here. For the six months leading up to your wedding, I'm putting you in charge of Special Wedding Operations and making you the Minister for Time Out. Even if all goes to plan, planning a wedding can be stressful at times and it's important for you and your Nearly-Wife to have a break from all things wedding-related and just enjoy being together. It's kind of like a 'date night' — once a month for the six months leading up to the wedding it'll be your job to organise a wedding-free zone.

This could involve dinner at a restaurant, an afternoon at the beach or the park, a night at the movies or even just good old pizza and DVDs on the couch in your bog-catcher tracky dacks. It doesn't matter what you do or how much it costs: what's important is that you set aside time to simply be together and enjoy each other without talking about anything to do with your wedding. Plan these time-outs with your Nearly-Wife in advance to ensure you're both free for them and don't break the dates. Trust me: as you progress with all your planning, each time-out will become a welcome oasis of calm and a light at the end of each month of 'Have you organised the cars yet?' 'Did you call the hire place about your suit?' and 'Have you made those hotel reservations or do I have to do them myself?'

If you really want to go the extra mile, schedule the last time-out for a few days before the wedding and make it something really special, like a his-and-hers massage at a day spa. The relaxation benefits will be fantastic for both of you and a great way to ease yourselves into the final countdown to the wedding.

The Accessories

When it comes to peripheral wedding accessories such as flowers, shoes and jewellery, the best advice I can give you is this: if you don't want to be charged a fortune for them, try to avoid mentioning they're for a wedding.

I'm serious – when people hear that something's for a wedding, this somehow becomes reason enough for them to jack up the price. Take florists, for example. When I was ringing around to get quotes for my bridal flowers I had a sneaking suspicion I was being ripped off so I did a simple experiment. I decided what sort of flowers I wanted in my bouquet and then rang a florist to ask how much a bridal bouquet containing those flowers would cost. A few days later I rang the same florist and asked how much a bouquet containing those same flowers would cost, with no mention of the bouquet being for a wedding. In fact, I said it was for a funeral. The bridal bouquet cost almost double what I was quoted for the 'funeral' bouquet. In fairness to florists, I know they can do a few extra things for a bridal bouquet like shaping the blooms or wrapping the stems, but almost *double*? Smells a bit pooey to me. I learned two lessons here:

1. Bridal isn't always better, and
2. You can get stuff cheaper if you say that someone's carked it. Apparently.

Bridal really *isn't* always better. Going to specialty bridal shoe and jewellery stores means you'll certainly see suitable shoes and jewellery but you'll also see gigantic price tags. If you've got the budget to spare, go for it. If not, shop around. You can often find suitable shoes and jewellery at general footwear and jewellery shops, both for you and for your bridesmaids.

For example, after spending more than I should have on my dress I was keen to save money on my shoes but I nearly wet my pants when I saw the price tags at specialty bridal shoe shops. Some of the shoes were gorgeous but they were all very . . . well, bridal. In the sense that they'd look great with a wedding dress but you'd be hard pressed to be able to wear them with anything else ever again. Determined to get more bang for my buck, I started looking at 'normal' shoe shops and ended up finding perfect little ivory satin slip-ons with a few diamantes and a mid-heel – for the delightful sum of $49.95. I shit you not. And do you know what I do with them now? Wear them practically every second weekend when I want to dress up my jeans. And when the shoes get dirty, I put them in a lingerie bag and throw them in the washing machine. Brilliant.

I found my bridesmaids' shoes at the same shop for $90. Two weeks later I saw an identical pair in a bridal magazine for $290. What the hell? Same goes for jewellery. I bought my bridesmaids' and flower girl's jewellery from Kleins and do you reckon anybody else at the wedding could tell that those pearls weren't the expensive ones you see advertised in all the in-flight magazines? Only a jeweller's going to be able to tell whether your bridal jewellery or your bridesmaids' jewellery is 'real' – save yourself a bundle and look at chain store or costume jewellery shops. The designs are just as good and they often have a much bigger range than the specialty shops. Chain stores are also really good if you're not looking for traditionally-styled jewellery and want something a bit different.

Jewellery Tips

- Don't expect your bridesmaids to pierce their ears just because you want them to wear a certain type of earring. Would you pierce your nipple just because your Almost-Husband wanted you hang a little bell off it? Okay, not quite the same but surely you catch my drift.

- If your bridesmaids don't have pierced ears, don't even bother with clip-on earrings. Clip-ons are for nannas and daytime soapie actresses (who for some reason always take an earring off when they talk on the phone – weirdos).

- If you or your bridesmaids are going to be wearing costume jewellery, make sure nobody's allergic to nickel. Seriously. A friend of mine had a bridesmaid who broke out in a severe rash because the skin on her chest reacted to her funky metallic necklace. She had to hold her bouquet in front of it while walking down the aisle and in photos.

- If you want to cut costs, keep jewellery simple. Less is more, anyway.

- Jewellery can be functional and symbolic as well as fashionable: I wore a silver dome-shaped locket that held six photographs. I digitally-scanned photos of my three grandparents who've passed away and The Bloke's three grandparents who've passed away. Shrinking the images down to size so they'd fit in my locket meant that all our grandparents could be with us on our wedding day. And all that was The Bloke's idea. Aww.

SHOE TIPS

- When shopping for footwear for yourself and your bridesmaids don't just think about what the shoes look like, think about what it's going to be like to wear them because you're going to be on your feet for a very long time and some of that time will include dancing. So those ten-inch heels you've got your eye on might look hot but trust me: your bridesmaids will want to stick them in your eye by the end of the night and those dance steps you took the trouble to learn will look nothing like they're supposed to when you try to dance without bloodflow to your toes.

- Beware of any slightly uncomfortable shoes that shop assistants tell you 'have a lot of give in them'. They don't. They just don't.

- Regardless of how comfortable your shoes are when you try them on in the shop, always wear them in and make sure your bridesmaids and your Almost-Husband do the same, to prevent painful blisters on your big day (or at least give you an idea of where to put the pre-emptive Band-Aids). The best place to wear in your shoes is around the house – this is so you don't get them dirty and also so you can laugh at what you look like in stunning shoes and bog-catcher tracky dacks.

- Scuff the soles of your shoes by putting them on

and dragging your foot along rough concrete or road a few times (the movement should be similar to what angry bulls do with their front hooves just before they charge). This will ensure that your shoes aren't slippery so you don't end up giving whoever's doing your wedding video a crack at Funniest Home Video of the Year.

- Practise your first dance or have your dancing lessons while wearing your shoes. This will not only help wear them in but it'll also get you used to the fact that you always dance a bit differently in different shoes.

- While wearing your shoes during dance lessons, buy a pair of white sports socks and put them on over your shoes. Cut out a hole for the heel to poke through and then cut out another patch under the ball of your foot. Sticky tape the sock to your shoe in these two areas so it stays attached. Doing this ensures that when your Almost-Husband steps on your toes during your lessons (and he will), his shoes won't leave marks on yours – really important if your shoes are white.

- If your shoes are covered in satin or any other fabric, consider waterproofing or scotchguarding them. Your heels will sink into the ground if you're having outdoor photos and you don't want them looking brown by the time you get to the reception. And always follow the instructions on waterproofing or scotchguarding sprays when using them on delicate fabrics.

- If your shoes have diamantes on them, paint the diamantes and the surrounding clasps with a couple of coats of clear nail varnish. This will not only ensure that the diamantes don't come loose at any stage but the smooth surface will also ensure that the hem of your dress doesn't catch on the clasps when you walk – really important if your dress is lace or satin, which are prone to showing pulled threads.

FLoweR TIPs

- Always ask to see a portfolio of the florist's bridal work. Better to get an idea of the quality of their bouquets beforehand rather than risk finding out they're not up to scratch when they arrive on your wedding day.
- La-di-da bridal florists are fabulous but smaller florists are often just as good and a lot cheaper. Provided they're qualified to do bridal arrangements, your local florist can probably do what you want at a fraction of the cost. Ask to see their portfolio.
- If you don't know much about flowers, buy a bridal flowers magazine. Yes, they do exist. Have a browse

and see what you like the look of – the pictures usually have captions explaining what all the flowers are so you can relay what you like to your florist. These magazines are also great to have on hand to explain the bouquet shape or look you want your florist to achieve.

- Once you know what you want in the way of bouquets, buttonholes, centrepieces, etc., shop around. Flower prices are generally consistent – it's the florist's professional fees that can fluctuate and you want to make sure you get the best price.

- Talk with your florist about whether you want your floral arrangements to have a formal or 'just picked' look. Do you want tightly-structured, rounded bouquets or something a bit more natural? Do you want only flowers or flowers and foliage? A good florist will advise you not only on the sorts of flowers they can put in a bouquet but also on the flowers that are best suited to the various bouquet styles.

- Flowers that are in season will be much cheaper than flowers that aren't in season and may therefore have to be sourced from interstate. Choose wisely.

- Taking a picture of your dress and/or the brides-maids' dresses is a great way to convey your style to your florist so they can design bouquets in keeping with that style. Similarly, taking in fabric swatches that your florist can keep is an excellent way to ensure he or she correctly matches the colour of your flowers. When I visited my florist I took a picture of my dress and a fabric swatch from it, plus one of my bridesmaids' dresses and their shoes and let her keep the lot for a week. I felt a bit ridiculous lugging all that stuff in but my florist absolutely nailed the colours as a result.

- One way to cut costs is to arrange for someone to collect your flowers from the florist on your wedding day rather than have them delivered, as the florist will charge you a delivery fee. And bear in mind that there will potentially be four delivery locations: one will be where you're getting ready on the day, one where your Almost-Husband is getting ready, one where your ceremony will take place and one where your reception will take place.

- You can also save money by asking for the stems of your bouquets to be left exposed – having them wrapped usually costs extra. If you're going for an overall natural look for your flowers, exposed stems look better anyway.

- If your wedding venue does ceremony or reception floral arrangements as part of their package, these can still be personalised. My venue did all-white arrangements but I ordered a few bunches of the same rose I had in my bouquet for these to be added to the centerpieces, thereby tying the venue's flowers into my floral theme. And no, I never thought I'd see the day when I'd be using the phrase 'floral theme' either.

BLOKE'S WORLD

Accessories

Let's be frank. Particularly if your name is, in fact, Frank. Here's the deal, Frank: I know you couldn't give a flying continental about flowers. Leave that to your Nearly-Wife. Just be sure to remind her of any floral allergies you might have that she's not already aware of. We can't have you covered in mucus on the big day.

So you know what to do with your buttonhole arrangements when they arrive on the day: they go on your left lapel. Check with your Nearly-Wife beforehand whether the stem is meant to point up or down because every arrangement is different.

As far as jewellery goes: again, probably not a big concern for you. Cufflinks should do it or maybe a tie-pin if you're being fancy. And I'm sorry but regardless of how hard you played to win it, last year's premiership medal is not considered appropriate wedding-day jewellery.

Make sure your shoes and your groomsmen's shoes are clean and super-shiny. And make sure your best man has the rings. A little hint: having him keep them in a little pouch that he can slip into his jacket or pants pocket is safer than having them in there loose.

THE GIFTS

They say it's the thought that counts when it comes to gift-giving but I beg to differ. I once gave a large, beautifully-wrapped box of thoughts as a wedding present and that couple still won't speak to me, despite the fact that I put happy thoughts in there and everything.

Some people go overboard when it comes to wedding gifts and nothing proves that more than a bridal registry. The argument is that bridal registries are practical because they guarantee you get the things you actually need instead of, say, six toasters. But what's wrong with six toasters? You could have one in every room of your house and never go without crumpets in the laundry again.

There are definite advantages to having a registry but no matter how practical you might feel telling people what you need, doing so takes all the fun out of gift-giving for your guests. Whenever a couple denies me the pleasure of setting them up with a complete set of at-home colonic irrigation equipment (let's think optimum bowel health, people!), I can't help but feel a little cheated.

Some people get a bit unhinged when it comes to choosing the items on their registry. By all means ask for what you like but don't get ridiculous. When two of my best friends got married one of their gift registry suggestions was a $370 sausage knife. Do yourself a favour and just read that sentence again. Now stop laughing.

Many a thought occurred to me off the back of that $370 sausage knife (so much so that I considered gift-boxing them for Mother's Day but once bitten, twice shunned). Who cuts that many sausages? Do sausages really need a separate knife? How many people have I embarrassed myself in front of by using the wrong knife to cut my sausage? Can a sausage knife be used to cut other processed meats? Who invented sausage knives? What colours do they come in?

Morally and literally, I didn't buy it. First of all, if I'm going to pay that much for a piece of cutlery I want guaranteed access to it at all times. I want to be able to phone my newlywed best mates at three in the morning and say, 'I need to chop some chorizo. Get dressed and I'll see you in five.'

Second, a wedding gift should mean something. It should remind the bride and groom – even years later

– of someone who attended their wedding. I don't particularly like the idea of someone thinking about me while they're cutting up sausages. Even worse if they're thinking, 'I can't believe she actually shelled out $370 for this!'

SHOULD I HAVE A GIFT REGISTRY?

While gift registries take all the thought out of gift-giving they can be extremely practical. If you're setting up a new home you should at least consider a registry because if you set one up at a homewares or department store you can pretty much kit out your entire house with your guests' help. Registries at furniture stores are also becoming increasingly common and so are 'His & Hers' registries, which involve the bride setting up a registry for things like manchester, glassware and crockery (totally 1950s housewife but understandable) and the groom setting up a registry for things like barbecues, hardware and outdoor furniture (man-heaven, apparently).

If you and your beloved have been living together for a while and you already have all you need on the domestic front, you might like to consider setting up a registry through a travel agency. These registries operate like a fund that your guests can contribute towards. You then get a record of everyone who's put in (so you can thank them later) and you end up with a pile of cash that you can put towards your honeymoon or another trip further down the track. It's a great idea if you've got enough stuff and you like the idea of taking a trip somewhere amazing and not having to foot the bill yourself.

Other popular gift registry ideas include those for wine (hello!), lessons (for golf, languages, cookery, etc.), experiences (such as scuba diving trips and hot-air ballooning, would you believe?), projects (such as a renovation or garden landscaping job) or art and antiques. I have heard of a wedding where the guests were asked to bring nothing more than their favourite recipe, which the couple planned to turn into a wedding cookbook. Another wedding I heard of involved the guests each bringing a plant that was suitable for the couple to transplant into their garden (to my knowledge, nobody brought a marijuana plant and I'll bet you the bridal couple were disappointed).

If you don't want any wedding gifts and would like to use your wedding as an opportunity to see that someone else gets something, you could organise charitable donations instead of gifts. Collecting money for a favourite cause or important charity such as cancer research or saving the purple-arsed hippo is a great way to make your wedding gifts keep on giving. As with all registry information, include your intentions with your invitation and liaise with your charity to ensure you can provide official donation envelopes to your guests at the reception.

Alternatively, you might like to set up a registry with a not-for-profit organisation that provides tax-deductible charity gift vouchers, such as Karma Currency. They're an Australian company that allows you to set up a registry exactly the same way you'd set one up at a department store, but instead of choosing the gifts you'd like your guests to buy, you choose the charities you'd like them to donate to. The registry then keeps track of who has donated to what so that you can send out thank you cards as you would for tangible gifts. Simple, helpful and more meaningful than a toaster. Or, as The Bloke said, 'Yes, but what good is it if I have to go all the way to Africa for a piece of toast in the morning?' I don't think he got it, either.

I'M HAVING A GIFT REGISTRY AT A STORE. WHERE DO I START?

Sit down with your Almost-Husband and make a list of all the things you need. For example, if you're setting up a new home you'll need things such as furniture items, bed linen, crockery, pots and pans, glassware, electrical goods, etc. A good way to figure out what you need is to divide your home into zones (kitchen, bathroom, laundry, bedroom, dining room, lounge room) and think of all the items you need to equip those zones.

Next, make a list of all the things you want. Remember that needing something and wanting it are different. The zoning process can also be of use here: consider each zone, look at what you've chosen to equip the zone and then consider what you'd like to decorate or finish it off. For example, you might have chosen a table for the dining room because you needed one: now consider things like placemats, napkins, candle-holders and the like. Similarly, you might have chosen bedlinen because you needed it: now consider things like a multi-setting electric blanket or a beautiful mohair throw.

'Want' items can also be just plain fun. If you've had your eye on a cool novelty corkscrew or your Almost-Husband has always wanted of those singing fish that you mount on the wall (oh, God) put them on your registry list. Registry items are gifts for you, not for your guests, so don't restrict yourself by only listing items that you think others would want to give you (I'm talking to you, aunty-who-thinks-every-couple-should-own-a-silver-tea-service).

GIfT REGISTRY TIPS:

1. Make sure your registry is set up before you send out your invitations for the people who go

shopping for gifts the day after they receive an invitation. Trust me. They're out there.

2. List items of various prices. Don't assume everyone spends what you spend on a wedding gift – try to cater for all budgets. The advantage of listing some lower-priced items is that there's something there for people who don't have much to spend. Similarly, listing a few big-ticket items means that a group of people who want to put in together to get you something really fancy are also able to do so. Everything else should fall somewhere in between.

3. It's your Almost-Husband's registry, too. This isn't your opportunity to just make a list of everything you've ever wanted. Make sure he has input by including items he wants, too, or at least give him a chance to help you decide what goes on the list. Respect his opinions and his taste and if he's not keen to deck the bedroom out in pink and lace, back off!

4. When it comes to a gift registry, more is more. Too few gift options and the guests who arrive at your nominated store only to find everything's already been purchased will be left thinking, 'Well what was the point of that?' As long as you're aware there's no guarantee you'll get everything you put on your list, make sure you put more items on the list than there are guests. I've heard that the general rule is three items of varying price per couple or single guest,

but good luck with that if you're having 250 people at your wedding!

5. Don't go overboard. A $370 sausage knife. Seriously.

IS IT oKAY To ASK foR MoNEY InsTEAD oF GIfTs?

All the rules of etiquette point to 'no' but the rules of etiquette also state that you shouldn't send gift registry information out with your invites but should instead wait for people to ask you what you want before you send them the info. And nobody does that.

The Bloke and I defied the 'don't ask for money' rule at our wedding. Being avid cooks who enjoy entertaining, we'd wanted to renovate our kitchen for ages but hadn't been able to afford it. We had everything else we needed for our house so instead of a gift registry we established a Kitchen Fund. We enclosed a separate gift card with our invitations and it stated the following:

We are fortunate enough to have everything we need, so to keep life simple we request no gifts. The most important thing is that you will be making our day special just by sharing it with us. However, we would really love to renovate our little house and any help would be truly appreciated, so if you'd like to contribute to our Kitchen Fund . . .

We set up an account for the kitchen, advised people of the account details so they could make a deposit instead of bringing cash to the wedding and that was that. This rocked the boat, let me tell you. A couple of people raised their eyebrows and suggested that this was 'unusual' (read: rude) but here's what I think: a gift should be about the recipient, not the gift-giver. How's asking for money any different to dictating a gift registry that tells your guest what to buy?

I've been to many weddings where the couple has asked for cash and personally, given the economic climate nowadays, I think it's okay. However, there are some important points to observe if this is what you're planning to do:

1. Don't just ask for money: let your guests know exactly what they're contributing to. Is it for a renovation? A home deposit? A caravan? A boat? People feel weird when they don't know where their money's going.

2. Be careful how you word your request. I once saw the phrase 'In lieu of gifts we are requesting cash' on an invitation and nearly threw myself out the window. The words 'cash' and 'money' should never appear in your request – it sounds really blunt. Try to find a nicer way to express your request. And always acknowledge that your guests' attendance is more important than what they give, which is true

no matter what you're doing for gifts.

3. Forget having a 'wishing well' (if you've never seen one, it's literally a little decorated well that's set up somewhere for guests to put cash into). Not only do wishing wells look naff but your reception venue will almost always insist you lock it to protect their liability. A padlocked well doesn't look too festive and your guests might feel affronted by it (the implication being that it's them you can't trust). Wishing wells also require your guests to bring cash to the wedding and physically donate it in front of everyone – something I think we'd probably all rather not do.

4. Respect your guests' right to not contribute or to insist on giving you an actual gift. Some people just aren't comfortable with giving money and others prefer to give a more traditional gift. Make a list of a few things you and your Almost-Husband need so you're prepared if someone insists on buying something.

5. Don't forget to thank people! After our wedding The Bloke and I sent cards to thank our guests for their generosity towards our fund and gave them an idea of when we planned to start the reno. Then, when it was all finished, we emailed 'before' and 'after' photos to them so they could see exactly how their generosity helped us.

BLOKE'S WORLD

Gift registries

I know – you'd rather wear something crotchless while riding a bicycle than traipse around a department store choosing butter knives. But organising your wedding gift registry doesn't have to be that bad.

On the contrary, it can be fun. You might not care about manchester initially (as well as an English soccer team, that also means towels and bed linen), but who says you're not going to discover the world's best quilt or the biggest, manliest towels on the planet?

If it's still sounding about as attractive as plucking your leg hairs individually, rest assured, a gift registry isn't just about stuff for the kitchen, bedroom and bathroom. Want a kick-arse barbecue? Put it on your registry. Need garden tools, hardware, a stereo or camcorder? Put it on your registry. Your wedding gifts should reflect your tastes and interests as much as they reflect those of your Nearly-Wife, and the best way to ensure that is to be part of the process when it comes to organising the registry list. Just make sure you follow the basic rule of making sure there are items of varying values so you cater for all budgets. And good luck convincing your Nearly-Wife that the two of you really need a Wii.

PARENTS

Wedding planning doesn't always run smoothly as far as parents are concerned. Most parents want to help out wherever they can and are usually full of ideas for your wedding: what you should wear, where you should marry, who you should invite, what your service should involve, what song they should warble drunkenly to you when they get on stage with the band in the wee hours of your reception.

Your parents' ideas are often based on what they did for their wedding or what was expected and accepted in their day. But times change and because of that, parents and their soon-to-be-married kids can sometimes end up butting heads over wedding plans. Throw in a few cultural differences if you and your beloved come from different ethnic backgrounds and there's every chance someone's going to end up drinking sherry before noon on a weekday.

My parents, Lia and George, married in a Greek Orthodox ceremony in 1975. Of the 220 people they had at their wedding, about 30 of them were their mates – the rest were family and friends invited by my grandparents. Some of these people were invited solely on the grounds that they had invited my grandparents to the weddings of their kids and, consequently, there were people at my parents' wedding that they'd never even met before. Talk about intimate!

While there's no doubt my parents enjoyed their wedding, it was also very much their parents' day. After I got married, Mum told me that the biggest difference between my wedding and hers was that every detail of my wedding was overseen by me and The Bloke, whereas most of the details of hers were overseen by my grandparents, in particular my mum's mum. Which is why I still think my mum was extremely lucky she didn't end up wearing a dress made of doilies and clear plastic.

I love my grandmother very much but her predilection for doilies and clear plastic borders on profound. Clear plastic covers nearly every surface of her home – including the hallway carpet – and until recently she also had doilies on the shelves in her fridge. Why the doilies? 'Because they're pretty.' And why the plastic? 'Because it protects'. My mum could have been the prettiest, most protected bride that ever lived.

While I was baptised under the Greek Orthodox faith I no longer practice that or any other religion and The Bloke isn't religious either, so we were never going to marry in a church. While I'm sure that this disappointed my folks, they had the good grace not to ark up about it. They were also great with our guest list: they only added two couples we hadn't initially included and they were more than happy with our final numbers being roughly half theirs.

So after avoiding arguments about the 'big' issues, I was convinced my parents and I would cruise through the wedding fuss-free. Turned out my parents and I were more into fussing over little things. The only disagreements we had were over pretty minor details, but little things can turn into big things. For me it was a matter of ensuring my wedding day remained about what The Bloke and I wanted for our big day, not what our parents thought was best. So the situation between my parents and me was kind of like that bit in the movie *Armageddon* where it becomes apparent that an asteroid is going to collide with the earth and fuck it up a bit.

For example, one of the things we argued about was the music at the reception. My parents wanted heaps of Greek dancing – imagine the wog version of *Saturday Night Fever* – but The Bloke and I wanted half an hour of the easiest Greek songs to dance to so that all the non-wogs could join in, followed by regular dance music for the rest of the night. (Note: I'm not being racist by saying wog, I'm being self-referential. In comedy circles this is widely known as the Steady Eddy defence.)

This argument went for just over a week – and here's what I mean about little things turning into big things – and it was the only part of the planning process that brought me to tears of frustration. Mainly due to the fact that I wanted to throttle my own mother.

I love my mum to the moon and back and admire her in so many ways, but she and I have always clashed because we're both as stubborn as each other. She may well have brought me into the world but I'll be honest: during the planning of my wedding, I toyed with the idea of taking her out. Basically, Mum wanted me to uphold a bunch of traditions that I wanted to throw out the window and note: this is often the root of pre-wedding arguments between parents and their soon-to-be-married kids.

So that you don't think your family is retarded if similar disagreements happen during your wedding planning, I'll give you an idea of what my mum and I disagreed over. When I said I wasn't going to walk down the aisle with my veil covering my face, Mum said, 'But it's traditional!', and then tried to change my mind. Repeatedly. When I said I wasn't going to throw my bouquet, Mum said, 'But it's traditional!', and then tried to change my mind. Repeatedly. So if you find yourself struggling with these sorts of petty disagreements with your folks, just arrange for someone to be on hand to yell out, 'But it's traditional!' and then try to make the best gin and tonic you've ever tasted. Repeatedly.

By the way, don't worry about my mum and me – we're totally fine now. Mum knows she gave me the shits but I gave her worse throughout most of my teenage years so we're probably even. We resolved our differences: the dancing issue went my way on the grounds that I was the one paying for the DJ. Mum let go of her veil-over-the-face issues after I said it would mean the world to me if I could wear her veil . . . on the condition that she let me remove the over-the-face bit, which she did.

And I got Mum a beauty on the bouquet-throwing issue. During all our disagreeing, I never actually gave her my reason for not wanting to follow tradition by throwing my bouquet – possibly because at the time, I was too busy researching hit-men. So you can imagine Mum's shock when I presented her and Dad with it during the wedding speeches as a token of my love and personal thanks for everything they'd done for me and The Bloke. It was the ace up my bridal sleeve and to be honest, I'll never forget the wonderful look of surprise on their faces and how good it felt for me to show, in front of everyone, how much they mean to me. And like I said: it got Mum a beauty!

If you're having 'issues' with your parents or soon-to-be parents-in-law, here are some useful points to remember:

1. Hear them out. Doing so gives you grounds to ask that they do exactly the same for you.
2. Rather than getting on a high-horse about not having to justify yourself because it's your wedding, explain why you feel the way you do. Give them a chance to see where you're coming from.
3. Always present a united front with your partner. This allows you to back each other up and be supportive of one another – good skills to practice for when you're married. Also, your parents may not be as inclined to be as insistent towards your partner as they are towards you, and the same with your partner's parents.
4. Be reasonable. Don't try to fight for something that you know is outside the realms of possibility, e.g. 'Mum, I told you we don't want a Catholic service – we want you to convert to Buddhism and perform the ceremony!'
5. If you're stuck at an impasse, try to find a compromise – without totally losing sight of what it is you're trying to achieve.

6. Thrashing it out with the folks is never fun but when it comes to the most important day of your life, it's often necessary. Don't allow yourself to be bullied into something you don't want just for the sake of avoiding an argument.

7. 'With all due respect' is a great phrase to use in your negotiations. Let them know they have your respect but make it clear that ultimately, the wedding is your day and you don't want to look back on it with regrets.

If the situation is still looking really dire, just photocopy and mail this letter from me:

Dear Parent-of-soon-to-be-married-son-or-daughter,

The following is a list of things your child would like to tell you but feel they are unable to say in relation to your involvement in the planning of their wedding.

Their inability to directly state these points may be because they love you and don't want to hurt your feelings (despite the fact that you're being a complete shit). It may be because they don't wish to offend you and thereby lose the cash you pledged towards the wedding. It may be because they're afraid you'll write them out of your will. Or it may be all of the above – let's not dwell. In any case, please observe the following in all future discussions regarding the wedding:

1. You may suggest. You may not insist.
2. Nobody likes a guilt trip.
3. Times have changed. Accept it.
4. At the end of the day this is not your wedding.
5. With all due respect, back the fuck off.

In the event that you fail to observe the above and continue to cause your child angst, let's just say: I know some people.

Thanking you for your co-operation,

Terri
Xx

Now, let's all have a drink!

PRENUPTIAL AGREEMENTS

Here's the thing, and this goes for brides and grooms-to-be: if you want to know how to go about arranging a prenuptial agreement you're going to have to ask someone else. Because, honestly, I just don't agree with them. Sorry, but I don't.

I was once amazed to read this in a bridal magazine wedding plan: 'Discuss a prenuptial agreement with your partner. They're quite common these days and protecting your assets will be a priority in the event that things don't work out.'

Firstly, what a great magazine: 'Congratulations! Here's hoping you don't get divorced!' Call me old-fashioned but surely getting married should be about looking forward to your future together, not thinking about what might go wrong and who'll get the house/car/labradoodle if it does.

And if prenups are indeed 'quite common' I'd love to know the real reason why. Like a lot of wedding-related stuff, I'm tipping there's a lot of 'I'll have what she's having' going on with prenups. You know the sort of flow-on effect I'm talking about: one couple in a friendship group has a stretch Hummer as their wedding car and suddenly all the couples in that friendship group have to have a stretch Hummer as their wedding car (although if you've ever seen a stretch Hummer you'll know that it's actually big enough to have as your wedding venue).

These flow-on effects have always been there when it comes to weddings. My parents were the first couple in their friendship group to marry. They chose to dress their groomsmen in powder-blue velvet suits and, thanks to the flow-on effect, all their friends now have wedding photos they're too embarrassed to show anyone.

One of my friends insisted on a prenup when she married because 'you never know what might happen down the track'. Ironic when you consider this is the same woman who had no qualms about building her home next door to a family who allow their teenage son to do 'science experiments' with flammable liquids in the shed.

I fail to understand how you and your partner can begin planning your married future while simultaneously drawing up a document that assumes that at some stage, one of you is going to call that future off. It's a bit like buying tap shoes for someone in a coma. Seems kind of pointless to me.

Considering a prenuptial agreement in the lead-up to your marriage automatically turns matters of the heart into a business transaction, and a grubby one at that. I hear 'prenup' and I think of leaving money on top of a chest of drawers while someone puts their clothes back on. It's just not what marriage has ever been or should ever be about. And an especially scorn-laden snort from me to the idea that prenups are a product of a modern or enlightened society. Frankly, anyone who thinks prenups are a symbol of modern life is getting them confused with muffin-tops. And I dare you to try to get your partner hot by showing them a hint of sexy prenup. Talk about a mood-killer.

I honestly can't imagine how you'd even begin to bring a prenup into conversation with your partner while maintaining you know anything about romance. 'Hey, you know how I said I love you more than life? And you know how I said you're all I need? And you know how I said I want us to spend the rest of our lives together? Yeah, well, I also want you to sign this document that says if all that goes to shit, you'll keep your stinking hands off my stuff.' Cue the Barry White music, I'm taking my clothes off already.

If you're worried about how you're going to divvy everything up in a divorce or you're concerned your partner might have gold-digging tendencies, here's a suggestion: don't marry them. If, immediately after a marriage proposal, your thoughts turn to the best way to divide assets there's every chance you've got your priorities wrong. There should be stars in your eyes, not dollar signs and you should be celebrating, not calculating. So what if Erica Baxter and James Packer signed a prenup? That wasn't about money. Everyone knows he just wanted to protect his impressive, if somewhat disturbing, collection of Speedos.

Ultimately, if you're reading this and you're still worried about the prospect of getting fleeced by your spouse, just do what I do and avoid being financially successful. Sure, you'll both end up cursing your lotto numbers week after week, but on the upside, you can't take half of nothing.

THE HENS' NIGHT

I'm not really into hens' nights because I've been to enough of them to know that they usually involve male strippers. Don't get me wrong: I have nothing against the naked male form. In fact, I'm quite the fan. But there's something a little bit not quite right about a guy who gets his cock out to the tune of Delta Goodrem's 'Out Of The Blue'. There's no subtlety there.

And I don't know about you but I kind of feel like if you've seen one stripper you've pretty much seen them all. And towards the end of a hens night with an all-male revue featuring six strippers one after the other, I tend to find myself thinking, 'Seriously. Unless this next dick has got antlers, I'm out of here. Six naked men and not one single dick trick? I've been ripped off.'

When one of my girlfriends got married she assured me that hers was going to be a 'classy' hens' night and by that she meant there'd be no strippers. But how classy a night do you reckon you're going to have when you rock up to a hens' night and the very first thing you're given is a drinking straw shaped like a penis? And I have to emphasise: not just any penis. Imagine for a moment the most offensive knob ever created since George W. Bush's parents conceived. This is what we were given and told we had to drink from. So much for a classy night.

The interesting thing about a penis-shaped straw – and I'm tipping that's not a sentence you read very often – is that once you've had an initial giggle at it, the novelty pretty much wears off (which can also be said of the real thing). At least, the novelty wore off for me – it didn't wear off for all the other women at the party. For some reason they felt obliged to try to keep the joke alive for the whole night. For example, when the woman sitting next to me at dinner excused herself from the table to go to the bathroom, she asked me to look after her drink with the phrase 'Don't touch my cock'. When she again needed the bathroom about twenty minutes later, she repeated the request. By this stage she was pretty pissed: she'd broken the seal and was going to the bathroom every five minutes, making sure I knew where I stood as far as her 'cock' was concerned each time. And I'm telling you, the 42nd time I heard 'Don't touch my cock', I snapped. 'Don't touch your cock? I'm going to smash your cock. I'm going to snap your cock in half, jam it up your arse and then watch you try and drink your Cosmopolitan out of it.' I had no patience for that woman whatsoever.

But the reward for 'best effort' as far as flogging that dead joke had to go to the woman who shoved a bunch of those straws into her hairdo and then went around telling everyone that she felt like a bit of a dickhead. And the only thing that saved this woman was the fact that she was actually the bride-to-be's 84-year-old grandmother.

I can honestly say that this nan fascinated me. She was quite old and frail, she was surrounded by a pile of penis paraphernalia and she wasn't fazed by it one bit. In fact, she went on to provide the highlight of the night because she got up and made a bit of a speech after dinner in which she said – and I quote – 'I'd like to thank you all very much for having an old duck like me here this evening, and it's just a shame I can't join you girls at the nightclub later because I've got my good undies on and I know I would have scored.' I decided right there and then that if I ever make it to 84, that's the kind of woman I want to be.

Towards the end of the night I tired of the penis-shaped straw and being unable to find a bin, I popped it into my handbag. Which was a big mistake. Because the next day I went to a family function and had a conversation with one of my older aunties about a particular website. When she asked me if I had a pen so she could write down the web address, what do you think I mistook for a writing implement as I fumbled around inside my handbag? If you've ever wondered what a 62-year-old woman might say when spontaneously presented with a small plastic penis, the answer is 'My goodness'.

So that's why I'm not particularly big on hens' nights, although I should point out that I've also been to a bucks' night – and no, I wasn't the entertainment. When a friend of mine invited me to his bucks' day I was flattered to be considered one of the boys but, at the same time, my initial reaction was very girly: 'What the hell do you wear to a bucks' day?' Knowing that my dad had been to a few bucks' turns over the years I gave him a call to ask what I should wear. His response? 'Nothing. Every woman I've ever seen at a bucks' do has been wearing absolutely nothing, except maybe nipple tassles.' So helpful. And can I tell you that upon hearing my own father use the phrase 'nipple tassles', a tiny little part of me died.

The bucks' day was actually okay: a day at the races followed by a catered barbecue at the best man's house. Nudity arrived late in the piece in the form of a buxom topless waitress. Actually, make that a pregnant, buxom topless waitress. At one point one the groom-to-be and I were talking to her and she said, 'I've just clocked over three and a bit months and this is my last nude job because I reckon I'm starting to show.' Ten points for honesty; none for eroticism.

When it came to our bucks' and hens' celebrations, The Bloke and I were keen to steer away from the standard 'last hurrah' and do something a bit more low-key. We planned a combined hens' and bucks' weekend a month before the wedding in Port Fairy, a little seaside town about 3 hours from Melbourne, with our immediate family, bridal party and a handful of our closest mates. No strippers. Partly because we didn't particularly want them and partly because apparently they'd have had to be summoned all the way from Geelong and, really, who can be bothered?

Nudity, however, was never far from the agenda. One of my favourite mates is renowned for getting his gear off. He streaked at my 21st, he's been known to appear randomly nude in the background of photos (if you browse through my photo albums, you can play a game I like to call 'Where's Willy?') and he was pants-down and belting out Billy Joel's 'Leningrad' while propping up the bar at my engagement party. That's the sort of stuff that builds a rep. Hence the most popular phrase of our bucks' and hens' weekend: 'Is Ed nude yet?'

The fact that his wife and child were present may have had something to do with him keeping his clothes on. Two couples brought their babies along to our weekend and rather than inhibiting the party atmosphere, they added to it. Despite what Child Services might have to say on the matter, the sight of my child-bearing friends at a pub with a spoonful of baby food in one hand and a pint in the other made me very happy. At The Stump, my favourite Port Fairy pub, the local patrons were so taken with the kids they did a spot of knee-bouncing, asked their names so they could enter them in the pub sweep and when they found out the parents were there for our bucks' and hens' celebrations, they bought us all a round. I'm now seriously thinking of bearing my own child just for the free drinks.

Our bucks' and hens' weekend had no inflated condom veils or wind-up jumping cocks and no lap-dancing or shaving the eyebrows of the unconscious. It was just lots of really good food and drink with a small circle of our nearest and dearest and a weekend that was very relaxing for everyone (one of my friends' babies was so relaxed that he chose to finally start sleeping right through the night – they were overjoyed).

Trends for bucks' and hens' celebrations have definitely changed and many people are choosing to forgo the stereotypical debauchery. Instead they're choosing activities they enjoy or that reflect their style or personality. Often, the celebrations are held during the day or over the course of a weekend. By all means go ahead and get a stripper if you want one (we've all been there) but here's a list of other options you or your Almost-Husband might like to incorporate into your celebrations:

- Motorcycle riding
- Hot-air ballooning
- Dinner and a show
- Winery tour
- Pole-dancing lessons
- Belly-dancing lessons
- Horse riding
- A day at the races
- Go-karting
- Sailing
- House boating
- Cocktail-making classes
- Four-wheel driving
- Paintball
- A cruise
- A catered cocktail party
- A poker night
- A pampering session, such as massage or beauty services
- Jelly wrestling
- Circus skills workshop
- Movie-making party
- Drumming workshop
- Dance lessons

(By the way, I'm serious about the jelly wrestling – there are companies who will either bring a jelly-wrestling show to you or provide you with all the equipment you need to hold your own. Brilliant.)

Don't have your hens' and bucks' celebrations the night before the wedding. At least one or two weeks before is better so you have time to recover. Don't forget to help out your maid of honour or whoever is organising your celebration by giving them a list of people you really want to be there. And don't hesitate to let them know if there's anything you really don't want to do or incorporate in your celebration: they might be in charge of all the planning but ultimately, what they're planning is supposed to be an event that you'll enjoy, not look back on with a cringe.

I'M WORRIED ABOUT WHAT MY ALMOST-HUSBAND'S GOING TO GET UP TO ON HIS BUCKS' NIGHT. WHAT CAN I DO?

Have a combined bucks' and hens' like I did so you can keep track of him at all times! Just kidding. We've all heard bucks' night horror stories but if you trust a man enough to marry him, surely you can trust him to have a night out with his mates. So you trust him but don't trust his mates? You're well within your rights to take them aside and lay down the rules, I reckon. However, bear in mind that your Almost-Husband still has a right to have fun with his friends and just because they go to see a strip-show or have a topless waitress doesn't mean he's going to cheat on you. The best advice I can give you is to talk to him about your concerns. If you're really worried, have your bucks' and hens' celebration activities on the same day and arrange to meet up somewhere together later that night. And don't forget to make it abundantly clear that if he cuts loose and does anything stupid that ends up with him behind bars, you won't be falling over yourself to make bail.

BLOKE'S WORLD

The bucks' night

Boobs. Boobs, boobs, boobs, boobs, boobs. Right, now that I've said what you're thinking, let me just remind you that your bucks' celebrations don't have to revolve around boobs (or any other part of the female anatomy).

Above, you'll find a list of activities that you can pursue in the name of bucks' entertainment (and that you'll no doubt find a way to add boobs to if you really want them). Below you'll find a list of my all-time greatest bucks' night rules:

- Thou shalt not allow anyone – male or female – to get anywhere near your wang.

- Thou shalt not get a tattoo.
- Thou shalt not let anyone shave or wax any part of your body.
- Thou shalt not break anything.
- Thou shalt not drive drunk or let any of your friends drive drunk.
- Thou shalt not do anything on the advice of anyone who says anything along the lines of 'Don't worry, nobody will ever find out'.
- Thou shalt not get arrested – your Nearly-Wife will *not* be in any hurry to make your bail. Don't ask me how I know.

Why should you follow these rules, I hear you ask? Because I said so, that's why. And also because you'll thank me later – I promise.

PART

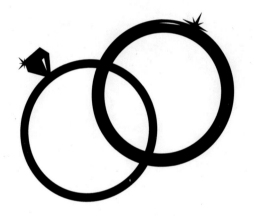

ThREE

The wedding day

THE CELEBRANT

If you're having a church wedding, finding a celebrant is easy: look for the guy in the robes who reckons he's good mates with God.

If you're not having a church wedding, you're in the market for a civil celebrant. Finding a civil celebrant is a bit trickier than you might think because unless you know one or someone recommends one to you, you literally have to shop around on the net.

The more I researched marriage celebrants the more I realised they're a very particular group of people. Next time you've got a spare ten minutes or you just want to look busy at work, google 'wedding celebrants' and I swear you'll notice the following about most of them:

- Middle-aged
- Foofy hair

- Big glasses
- Soft-focus photography
- The name Barbara

The Bloke and I had a look at all the celebrants on the net and then shortlisted a few people we wanted to meet with. And thank God we did that instead of just booking someone straight off the bat, because a lot of these people seemed okay on their webpages but in person they were often – how can I put this? – complete and utter nutbags.

For example, one of the celebrants cancelled herself out of the running mere minutes after we met her. All we did was walk into her office, introduce ourselves and shake her hand. Then, as we were making ourselves comfortable in our chairs she exclaimed, 'You know, the weirdest thing just happened. Just before you guys got here I pulled a huge boog out of my nose and my ear unblocked!'

It didn't matter what she said after that, she was out. We didn't want to run the risk of her pulling boogs at our wedding.

For some reason, all the celebrants I shortlisted cancelled themselves out when we met them. After boog-lady we met another woman who, for some reason, we got talking about star signs with. At one point in the conversation she was talking about Cancerians. I asked her what comes after Cancer. She exclaimed 'Remission!', then pissed herself laughing. So she was out.

Which left us with the only celebrant The Bloke had shortlisted and he shortlisted this guy for a very specific reason. While I had shortlisted celebrants because of things like the sort of ceremony they offered and the experience they had, The Bloke simply chose a celebrant on the grounds that his name was Barry.

I was sceptical at first but Barry won me over in the interview. Mainly because he told us a dick joke and a joke about anal within the first ten minutes of our meeting him. And I'll be honest, he had me at the dick joke. That's just the sort of person I am. I heard the punchline, turned to The Bloke and said, 'This is the guy.'

Sadly, Barry didn't work out to be quite as blue at our wedding but the thought of him peppering our ceremony with any mention of 'bell-ends' or 'back passages' still makes me quite wistful.

How Do I choose A celebrant?

Shop around for one on the net – most wedding celebrants list themselves on wedding directory websites or the official website of the Australian Association of Authorised Marriage Celebrants – www.marriagecelebrants.org.au

View a few profiles in order to try and get a sense of what the celebrant is like. It'll feel a bit like online dating but thankfully, most marriage celebrants don't post fake photos or lie about their cup-size and bedroom skills.

When assessing the celebrants at this stage, look for information about the kinds of ceremonies they offer. Many celebrants deck their websites out with ceremony samples (kind of like urine samples but more romantic). The ceremony samples will often give you a good idea of the celebrant's style. Are their ceremonies schmaltzy? Sternly-worded? Over-the-top? Boring as bat shit?

Eliminating the styles of ceremony you don't like is a great starting point when looking for a celebrant. But don't forget to bear in mind that many celebrants these days allow you to have lots of input into your ceremony, even more than just your vows (although there are some paragraphs and phrases that are actually required by law).

Pick two or three celebrants and arrange to meet with them in person. This is where you'll really make up your mind because you'll either 'click' with them or you won't, in which case keep looking. It's important to find a celebrant both you and your Almost-Husband like. Your celebrant will be more than just the person who performs your ceremony: they'll also set the mood for your whole wedding. How easy will it be for you or your guests to relax during the ceremony while you're all being boomed at by a wanker with some sort of pole stuck up his arse? Much better to find a celebrant whose personality complements yours and is therefore more likely to make your ceremony reflect who you and your Almost-Husband really are.

I'VE CHOSEN A CELEBRANT. NOW WHAT?

When you've found a celebrant you like and who you're confident will provide you with the ceremony you're after, book them and ask them to double-check that they haven't already been booked by someone else (seriously, it happens). Then ask them what documentation (usually a birth certificate) you need to provide them with and when you need to provide it. Doing this from the get-go will save you time and worry later, particular if you don't have a copy of your birth certificate. These can often take a while to obtain and it's no good realising you need one two days before your wedding. Ditto with lodging the official, legal documentation that indicates your intent to marry: fill this out with your celebrant, lodge it and cross it off your list of things to do.

Once you and your celebrant have this sorted, things can then go one of two ways: if you're happy to have little or no input into your ceremony, you can relax and let your celebrant do all the work. However, even if you're happy for them to compose every word I would strongly advise that you ask them to send you a draft of the ceremony for you to look over before your big day. That way, if they're planning on quoting lyrics from Meatloaf somewhere in the vows you can step in (unless of course you love Meatloaf, in which case I wish you and your mullet the best of marital luck and good day to you, madam).

If you want creative input into your ceremony you'll have homework to do. Ask your celebrant to send you a 'skeleton' of the ceremony to show you the order in which the various parts take place, then choose which bits you'd like to compose and which bits you're happy for your celebrant to take care of. For example, you might only want to write your own vows or just the vows and the ring exchange. Let your celebrant know what you'd like to compose yourself and be sure to consult with them regarding the parts of the ceremony that you are legally required to include – there are some sections that the celebrant and the couple must say a certain way in order for the marriage to be recognised as legal.

Don't be afraid to be particular when it comes to the words in your ceremony because these are some of the most meaningful words that will ever come out of your mouth. Think about them. Consider the promises you and your Almost-Husband want to make to each other in your vows and what you want to express to each other in front of all your friends and family. And don't be afraid to make it funny or personal: this ceremony will be completely yours and the more you put into it, the more unique and memorable it will be.

The Bloke and I were complete control freaks when it came to our ceremony and wrote pretty much every word except for the legal bits and Barry's welcome and introduction. Actually, let me rephrase: I was a complete control freak, The Bloke was just anti-cheese. He was strongly against any mention of soppy phrases like 'cupid's arrow' and 'the mystery of love' while I felt very strongly about us being the ones to write the words that would form the foundations of our marriage. I also wanted to include an appropriation of a Greek wedding tradition known as the Stefana (wedding crowns) to honour my heritage, so being able to have input into our ceremony was really important.

Barry was awesomely cool with this set-up. The Bloke and I wrote an initial ceremony draft, which Barry then sent back to us with some suggestions and we went back and forth via email about three or four times, drafting the ceremony like an essay. It took a bit of work to get it right but Barry's guidance was spot on and the end result was a ceremony that was completely 'us' and everything we wanted it to be. And without wanting to sound soppy, sitting down with The Bloke and a glass of red and working out the beautiful things we wanted to say to each other was one of the highlights of planning our wedding. Okay, now spew.

QUESTIONS TO ASK YOUR CELEBRANT:

1. How much input can you have into the ceremony?
2. Will you have to sign your wedding certificate with one of those ridiculous feathered quills that even Dumbo wouldn't be caught dead with?
3. Will your celebrant be available for a rehearsal and will this incur an additional fee?
4. What will your celebrant wear to your wedding? (This ensures they don't rock up in something ghastly. The men are usually okay because they wear a suit – it's the female celebrants you want to check out so they don't upstage your mum.)
5. Will your celebrant be performing any other weddings on the day? (A celebrant who has another booking is a risk – you don't want them being late to your ceremony or rushing through it to get to another one.)

BLOKE'S WORLD

I'm settling the argument for you now: the best celebrant is not necessarily the one with the biggest tits, so just drop it. That is all.

THE CEREMONY

There are many ways to personalise your wedding ceremony. If you're having a civil service you can write virtually the entire ceremony yourself like The Bloke and I did but even a church service can be personalised with the inclusion of readings that you and your Almost-Husband have chosen.

Readings can form an important part of a civil or religious service by reflecting ideas about love or marriage that are meaningful to you and your Almost-Husband. And contrary to popular belief, they don't have to be soppy, greeting-card bullshit. You know the sort of crap I'm talking about: all that 'recipe for love' malarkey with the 'Take a cup of love, add a pinch of tenderness, sprinkle with some patience and mix with lots of cuddles . . .' Always sounds like they're cooking up spew-cake to me.

If you want to include readings in your ceremony (and it's by no means compulsory), the words you choose can come from just about anywhere. You can use anything from song lyrics, extracts from novels or any other literature, extracts from philosophy books, extracts from children's books, dialogue from a film, famous or not-so-famous poetry, traditional blessings – the list goes on. If you don't already have a reading in mind, searching for wedding readings, lyrics, dialogue, etc., on the internet is a great place to start because you'll find heaps. Sure you'll have to wade your way through a lot of tripe but you'll also find some really beautiful words that will hopefully strike a chord. Just don't make the same mistake I did and start reading through them when you're pre-menstrual: I started reading at lunchtime and was a sobbing, blubbering mess by the time The Bloke got home that night.

When you've chosen a reading that you and your Almost-Husband *both* like (don't be a ball-breaker just because he doesn't care for *Winnie The Pooh* like you do), decide who you would like to deliver the reading during the ceremony. This could be anyone from your parents or another relative to a close friend, the person who introduced the two of you or even any children you and your Almost-Husband may already have – provided they're old enough to read confidently and mature enough not to use their big moment as an opportunity to announce the word 'fuck' into a microphone for no reason other than the fact that everybody's watching and it's fun to see Mummy and Daddy's faces contort with a mixture of total mortification and rage.

For our ceremony reading, The Bloke and I asked a married couple we're really close to to read an extract from the Greek philosopher Plato, because we're wankers. Just kidding. While writing my first solo Comedy Festival show, *Available*, I did a bit of research into the idea of soulmates and stumbled across an extract from Plato's *Symposium* where he talks about the notion of finding your 'other half'. I immediately loved his theory and when The Bloke and I had been together for long enough that I was sure he wouldn't laugh at me, I told him about it. He immediately laughed at me, but when the time came for us to choose a reading we both agreed that the extract from Plato was the one for us.

VoWS

The extent to which you can personalise your vows depends on the kind of wedding ceremony you're having. If you're having a religious service there's often little opportunity to compose or alter the vows but you'll know more about your particular religion's policy on that than I do.

Civil ceremonies allow for a lot more flexibility and creativity as far as vows are concerned: you can write pretty much whatever you want and be as serious, funny, simple or eloquent as you like. If you've chosen a celebrant who's happy for you to write your own vows they should be able to give you some examples from ceremonies they've performed in the past, as well as some guidance and workshopping time. And, of course, the internet is a fantastic resource for getting ideas when it comes to writing your own vows. Whether you blatantly rip off someone else's vows or mix and match them with your own is up to you but it's certainly a great starting point for some inspiration (and laughs – some of the schmaltz that's out there is hilarious).

Writing your own vows can seem like a daunting task at first but don't let that put you off doing it. It's actually not that difficult provided you have some time to think about it, and making your own promises in your own words is such a satisfying and meaningful thing to be able to do. It took a while to get them right but The Bloke and I were really proud of ours.

Essentially, your wedding vows are simply a statement of the promises that you and your Almost-Husband intend to uphold throughout your marriage. A great way to begin the process of writing your own vows is for both of you to have a think about all the qualities you think are important to a good marriage and the things you'd like to promise each other. The Bloke and I did this in a really simple way: we brainstormed. We literally just sat down over a glass or three of wine and came up with a list of words and phrases that we liked and that we thought were reflective of how we felt about each other and then used that list as a basis for our vows. The list was so helpful because it formed a starting point and focus for our promises and meant we didn't have to try to just randomly pluck them out of the air.

To help you and your Almost-Husband get going, here's a list of good words and phrases for vows:

- Nurture
- Care
- Respect
- Adore
- Best friend
- Cherish
- Encourage
- Trust
- Understand
- Affection
- Warmth
- Build a life
- Partner
- Support
- Faithful

- Comfort
- Unconditional
- Respect
- Honour
- Grow old together
- Loyal
- Devotion

And in the interests of balance, here's a list of words and phrases you might like to avoid:

- Celibate
- Confront
- Prostitute
- Ignore
- Ridiculous
- Suffocate
- Secret past
- Nag
- Debt
- Annoy
- Get a life
- Congenital defect
- Closet
- Mistake
- Venereal
- Antagonise
- Fetish

- Bludgeon
- Sex change
- Regret
- Bulbous
- Police record
- Collingwood

OThER wAYS To PeRSoNALiSE YoUR cEREMoNY

Aside from choosing the readings and writing your vows, there are a few other parts of your ceremony you can put a personal stamp on. Choosing your own music immediately personalises your service (see The Music, page 254) and you can also choose to incorporate any of a number of non-denominational or religious wedding rituals and traditions, including:

- Candle-lighting ceremony
- Ring-blessing ceremony
- Broom-jumping ceremony
- Sand, water or tea-pouring ceremonies
- A congregational promise
- Bread-breaking ceremony
- Flower ceremony
- Hand-tying ceremony
- Circling ceremony

- Wine-sharing ceremony
- Glass-breaking ceremony
- Crowning ceremony

The Bloke and I incorporated the Stefana into our ceremony and also had a ring-blessing ceremony (ha, ha). This involved our wedding bands being passed around for each of our guests to bless at the beginning of the service in the hope that they would be warmed by everyone's good wishes by the time they were returned to us to place on each other's finger. Depending on the wedding ritual you choose (if any – again, they're not compulsory), your civil or religious celebrant will be able to advise you of how best to incorporate it into your ceremony.

Other ideas for personalising your ceremony include choosing who's going to walk you down the aisle. Traditionally this honour was always left to the bride's father but more and more brides are choosing to be escorted by both parents, a close sibling, relative or even any children they may already have. A tip for you if you're going to be escorted by more than one person: make sure your aisle is wide enough. Both my parents walked me down the aisle and we asked our venue coordinator to move the seating on either side so we wouldn't be jostled or tripped up by furniture.

Similarly, you can also choose who you have as your official marriage witnesses. Again, tradition dictates that the best man and maid/matron of honour fulfill this task but legally, anyone over 18 can do it. The Bloke and I asked our grandmothers to witness our marriage and they were both so pleased and excited to do it. (My grandmother's first language is Greek and because her name is actually the only thing she can read or write in English, she was so nervous about signing our marriage certificate that she spent a couple of days before the wedding practising. Cute.)

BLOKE'S WORLD

The ceremony

If you're into the idea of creating a unique, non-namby-pamby wedding ceremony with your Nearly-Wife, I like the cut of your jib. However, please observe the following:

- Club songs, *Penthouse* letters and power-tool instruction manuals are not considered appropriate ceremony readings.
- Asking Gazza/Wazza/Macca/Donk to do a reading based solely on the grounds that he does really funny foreign accents is not necessarily a good idea.
- Promises regarding the regular performance of any sexual favours do not belong in your wedding vows.
- A 'tinny-cracking ceremony' is not a recognised wedding ritual.

THE VENUE

You can have your wedding ceremony and reception pretty much anywhere these days. If you're religious, a church is fairly standard for the ceremony but most civil celebrants will perform ceremonies wherever you like. Barry (the celebrant who married The Bloke and me) once performed an underwater ceremony. I'm not joking.

We were sitting in his office when we noticed a newspaper cutout showing a photo of a bride and groom being married underwater. Barry made a joke about nervous farting being hard to hide underwater due to air bubbles and then told us he was the celebrant in the photo. Apparently he happened to mention to the couple that he shared their love of diving and suddenly they were planning an underwater ceremony. I know: underwater weddings and jokes about anal and farts. How much cooler does this guy get?

As far as the reception goes, it all depends on the size of your guest list and the sort of wedding you want to have. Will your wedding be small or large? Will it be formal or informal? Do you want a traditional dinner reception, a wedding lunch or a cocktail reception? Do you want to get married locally or do you want a 'destination' wedding, where you and your guests escape somewhere for overnight or longer to get married by the ocean/in the hills/overseas/up a tree?

According to my dad, finding a venue for my wedding was simple. Dad's idea was that we should do what we did for my 21st and just 'throw a few tarps over the backyard'. When I pointed out that maybe we were looking for something a bit classier, Dad's response was, 'Then we'll borrow your uncle Noel's tarps – they're silver.' True story.

The idea of having the wedding at my parents' place brought back horrible memories from my 21st. On the day of my party Dad and I were setting up the backyard and we had a massive argument after I came round the side of the house and found him digging a hole about a metre wide and half a metre deep. When I asked him what he was doing he said he was digging a latrine for the male party guests to piss into.

When I asked him why, Dad said that everybody knows that if guys are at a backyard party they'll always have 'a little picnic-wee' somewhere in the yard rather than go inside looking for a bathroom, and he would much rather build them a 'designated pissing area' than have them turn my mother's entire rose garden into a 'piss-trough'.

We had a huge fight about this, standing in the backyard yelling at each other (there's no such thing as a quiet discussion in my family). I told Dad a latrine was ridiculous, he told me he'd been to enough backyard parties to know it wasn't. I said that just because he'd pissed in a few backyards didn't mean that's what my mates would do. He said I should put myself in my mother's shoes and think about how I'd feel if I bent down to sniff a rose and got a big whiff of wee. I said what would people think of us if they came to our house and saw that we had a backyard pissing area? Dad said what would they think of us if they came to our house and didn't see one?

In the end Dad abandoned the idea after I got really upset and told him I felt like he was insulting me by suggesting my male friends didn't know how to behave. That night at the party those male friends repaid me by pissing all over my mum's roses and doing a nudie run in front of my grandmother, who still remembers it*. So if my 21st was anything to go by, if I chose to have the wedding at Mum and Dad's place, tarps would be the least of my worries (although now I know why they had portaloos at the bridal expo).

---

*(and, yes, it was Ed.)

So we scratched the folks' place from the venue list and started looking at other options. For a while we flirted with the idea of getting married in Port Fairy. The Bloke has family links and a holiday home there and it's special to us because it's been the location for many happy times but, unfortunately, we had to scratch Port Fairy from the list too.

Firstly, when we ran the idea of a wedding that involved an overnight stay past my parents, Dad said, 'You can't do that. Your Aunty Mary would never leave her cat overnight – it's got diabetes.' Yeah. Because we were really going to plan the most important day of our lives around an 89-year-old woman's diabetic cat. Fuck it – let's have it at her house.

Secondly, Port Fairy lost out because of its lack of hairdressers. I'm serious. I know I told you I'm not a girly-girl but there's only one hairdressing salon in that area and I had a big problem with it, mainly due to the fact that it's called 'Men Only'. The Bloke couldn't understand my concern. Apparently I should have jumped at the opportunity to have my hair done in any style for only twelve bucks.

We finally settled on the Dandenong Ranges (because we like all that rainforesty bullshit) so we organised a little daytrip to start inspecting venues. Initially we were only going to visit three of them but after we realised that most of the venues give you a free bottle of wine when you go, we went on to visit another seven. It was time-consuming but a great way to stock our wine rack.

The free bottle of wine was my first indication that weddings are big bucks. To you and your Almost-Husband, it's the most important day of your lives. To the people in the wedding industry, it's big business and they'll do anything to try to get your cash.

For example, many venues try to have at least one special feature that sets them apart from all the rest. And when I say 'special feature', what I really mean is 'crock of shit'. Some of the special features of the venues we visited included – and I'm not making this up – a smoke machine and a laser light show.

The smoke machine blew so much smoke it could have killed a mild asthmatic. Although, on the upside, it would be great if you were feeling a bit depressed because the amount of smoke this thing would have been able to blow up your arse would be amazing.

The venue with the light show tried to demonstrate it for us *during the day*. Firing up a laser light show in broad daylight is like playing Twister with a multiple amputee. A bit pointless, really.

Out of all the venues we saw, my favourite was the one that actually had the least features – they just had an employee who was trying really, really hard. She was all of about 19 years old, she looked and smelled massively hung-over (which I respected) and she gave us this spiel as part of our tour: 'This is the bridal lounge, which is a private area where the two of you can come to get away from all your guests.' Because of course you want to get away from the people you've specifically invited to share your big day.

But she got even better: 'Now you'll notice the bridal lounge is quite large, quite comfortable and there are a number of special features: a nice couch, your own private bathroom and a box of tissues for any emergencies.'

What sort of emergencies? What was she talking about here – some sort of Monica Lewinsky moment with the dress? That would have to be it. Because if it was anything worse than that – if I spewed, if The Bloke spewed or god forbid, we shat ourselves – we were probably going to need more than just a Kleenex.

Funnily enough, that's the venue we ended up choosing. It was perfect for all our ceremony and reception needs ... and we liked the look of their tissues.

How To choose A cEReMoNY vENUE

Get a rough idea of guest numbers and then decide where you'd like your ceremony to take place. If it's all going to happen in a church, book it as soon as possible and then you only have to worry about your reception. If it's a civil ceremony, decide whether you want a separate ceremony and reception location or whether you'd prefer what I like to refer to as a 'one-stop wedding'.

This is what The Bloke and I had. Our wedding venue was basically a reception centre with a chapel on-site. We really liked this because it meant that our guests only had to attend one location – they didn't have to go somewhere for the service and then kill a few hours before they had to travel somewhere else for the reception. Note that 'kill a few hours' between a wedding ceremony and a reception can often mean 'get horribly drunk at a pub on the way' so bear that in mind if you want a genteel reception that doesn't include drunken behaviour (whatever). Our guests were able to go straight from the ceremony in the chapel to a big group photo outside and then into the foyer of our reception venue for pre-dinner drinks while we spent an hour having photos taken with our wedding party on the grounds.

Not only was this the easiest option for our guests but it was also terrific for us because it meant we didn't have to travel anywhere either. Instead, we were able to spend the time that we would have spent travelling mingling with our guests before the official reception. This also meant that the only wedding transport we needed was to get us from home to the ceremony – we didn't need the drivers to hang around during the ceremony, take us to our photo location, hang around for our photos, then take us to the reception. When you're paying an hourly rate for your wedding transport, a one-stop wedding can save you a bundle of cash as well as make your day and your guests' day so much easier. Translation: brilliant.

Regardless of whether you're one-stop-marrying or having a separate, non-church ceremony, an investigative mission to suss out ceremony locations is a must. For outdoor locations such as parks, gardens or the beach, you almost have to think like you're mapping out a location for a movie: where will the celebrant and bridal couple stand for the ceremony? Where will the guests be? Where will you enter the location from? Where will the 'aisle' be? What will be in the background as your guests are watching the ceremony? Is there shelter in the event of heat or cold? Will the ground support seating for guests or will everyone have to stand? What infrastructure will you need to provide – chairs, marquee, gazebo, table, red carpet, audio equipment?

Another important thing to consider is how windy the location gets. Wind can spell trouble for weddings, and I'm not just talking about nervous farting. Strong winds can play havoc with hairstyles, veils, short and flippy bridesmaids' dresses, the celebrant's script and keeping your marriage certificate in one spot when you're trying to sign it. It can also literally blow all the words of your ceremony away to the point where your guests can't hear them, regardless of whether or not you're using a microphone during your ceremony. How pissed off would you be if you spent hours writing your own vows only to overhear someone at the reception say, 'What a lovely service. Of course, I couldn't hear a damn word they were saying.'

If you decide on an outdoor ceremony on public land such as a park or beach, you'll need to contact the local council to advise them of your plans and obtain permission to use the area. The council will also let you know if there are any fees involved and whether or not your wedding date clashes with any other events happening in the vicinity that might affect your ceremony. Nothing kills the mood of an intimate Botanical Garden wedding ceremony quicker than 923 competitors sweating their way past in a fun-run.

Be as creative as you like when it comes to considering where you want your ceremony to take place. Wineries, fancy hotels, boats, hot air balloons, cliff-tops (wind!) – the choice is yours and providing the location meets your requirements, the possibilities are endless. Rollercoaster ceremony, anyone?

How To choose A Reception vENUE

The Bloke and I might have gone overboard in an effort to score free booze but visiting a few different places is crucial when it comes to finding your reception venue. Get started as soon as possible – some venues are booked out a year or more in advance and if you've got your heart set on securing a particular date you'd best get in early. Browsing through venues on the internet is a great way to start the hunt but it's important to actually go there and check them out too, because a website can only show so much.

Start by making a list of places you're keen to check out and then call to arrange a visit. Calling beforehand is essential in most cases – more often than not you'll want to do your inspections on the weekend and more often than not the venue will be hosting a wedding on the weekend. You can't just rock up and perve around the place while someone's getting married. Making an appointment ensures that you can poke around to your heart's content (usually in the morning before any weddings start) and it also ensures that someone from the venue will be there with enough time to give you a proper tour and answer all your questions – especially those regarding prices.

Don't be afraid to ask for references. Get a list of a few of the venue's most recent weddings, including the bride and grooms' contact details. Being able to get the low-down on things like food and service straight from the horse's mouth (so to speak) will give you a terrific idea of how a venue actually runs on the day, from the perspective of people who've been in the shoes you're about to fill.

There's a lot to consider when looking at a prospective reception venue. Firstly, is it big enough to comfortably hold all your guests? Making a rough guest list at this stage is a good idea because it will ensure you only look at the right sized venues for your needs. Find out how the venue actually seats people, e.g. how many guests to a table and how closely the tables are arranged, because this will give you a sense of how the night will feel – there's a big difference between cosy and cramped. You might also take into account the size of the dance floor for the same reason and if you're having a band, consider how much room the venue has for one. You might be rapt with the fact that you're having a nine-piece Latin band but your nan might not appreciate the fact that due to the venue not being big enough, the guy playing the maracas is sitting on top of her.

Does the decor of the venue suit your style and if not, is there flexibility to add or subtract what you may or may not want? Obviously they're not going to re-paint the walls or do a complete refurbishment for you but a good venue should be open to suggestions and willing to help you achieve your look. For example, I wanted lots of candlelight at my wedding but the venue only provided a few candles on each table. After a discussion with the venue coordinator, I was able to purchase about a hundred tea-light candles and candle-holders from Ikea (so cheap!) and organise for the venue staff to arrange them exactly where I wanted them throughout the chapel, the pre-dinner drinks foyer and the main reception area. (I drew them a scale diagram. Control freak? Not much.) The coordinator liked the result so much he even offered to buy the candle-holders from me after the wedding. I briefly considered jacking up the price but the guy had been so good to us that I ended up giving them to him for nix as a thank-you for helping us out with our big day.

By the way, your reception venue doesn't always have to be a reception centre. Restaurants can be also hired for weddings and one of the best wedding receptions I've ever been to was on a boat that cruised around Sydney Harbour. Again, be as creative as you like. In Victoria, for example, you could choose to have your reception at the aquarium or the zoo, in a pub or castle, at a winery or golf course, or at a restaurant, hotel or heritage estate. Your main objective should be to choose a venue that both caters to your number of guests and reflects your style and personality.

BLOKE'S WORLD

Choosing a venue

If you think you're not going to have to do any of the leg-work involved in finding a venue for your ceremony and reception, you're dreaming. Sorry to burst your bubble but I told you I'd be honest.

Your Lady might do the bulk of the scouting-for-things-on-the-net work, but you should definitely visit the venues with her. Be prepared to give up a few weekends in front of the telly in order to do a few on-site inspections. Yes, you can be the one to drive if you must and you can even stop off for a beer somewhere during your travels – trust me, you'll both need a drink after you've seen your 100th candelabra.

It's important that you take an active role in choosing where you'll marry and celebrate. If not, don't blame me when you end up with somewhere totally pink and full of cherubs.

The mother of all 'before' shots.

VENUE COORDINATORS / WEDDING PLANNERS

To put it bluntly, you might find yourself a brilliant venue but if the staff you're going to be dealing with during the planning process and on your actual wedding day are incompetent arseholes, you'll be in for a bumpy ride. If the venue has an in-house coordinator, meet with them when you inspect the venue to discuss your needs and try to get a sense of whether you think they're on your level. You don't have to like them so much you want them in your wedding party but it's important that you get along and that you're confident they can help you see all your plans for the day through to fruition. Having said that, I loved my venue guy. He was wickedly funny and more camp than a row of tents. He was also ridiculously good at his job and I liked the fact that when I mentioned that I thought the tradition of the garter-toss was a bit naff, he said, 'Bugger naff – I think it's completely rank.' My kind of straight-talking guy.

A good venue coordinator will also have ideas for your reception that you may not have thought of. Our venue guy suggested personalising our pre-dinner drinks with a signature cocktail. Known as The Watsonian, in honour of the suburb where The Bloke and I live, it consisted simply of a glass of sparkling white wine with a wild hibiscus flower added to it. These flowers come in little jars of rhubarb red syrup and turn your glass of bubbles a deep, sweet scarlet and the flowers actually open up as they absorb the alcohol. Impressive, delicious and incredibly simple, they confirmed our suspicions that our venue coordinator was, in fact, a complete genius.

He also helped us by giving us a complete list of wedding service providers (florists, photographers, DJs, etc.) that he thought were topnotch. This gave us a really easy starting point when it was time to case out those services, so make sure you ask for one too. From our first meeting with our coordinator, he understood that we wanted a no-fuss, minimum-formalities night and ensured that everything we planned reflected that. But most importantly, he made it clear that we would have unlimited access to him by phone and via email during the entire planning process. This was terrific because it ensured that we had plenty of time to come up with and explain our ideas. We could also ask any questions and check on things to make sure that everything was going according to plan. Beware of any venue coordinator who tells you you'll have one or two 'planning meetings' and that's all – that's not a coordinator, that's a lazy-arse.

As far as professional wedding planners go, I'll tell you this: they're bloody expensive. If you can afford one and you think you'd benefit from their expertise, go for it. Personally I reckon half the fun is planning things yourself and if you've got a decent venue coordinator you probably don't need any extra help. Having said that, if you're pressed for time (shotgun wedding, anyone?), a professional wedding planner can save you hours of work and dozens of frowns worth of anxiety.

ON THE DAY

On the off chance that you haven't already picked up on how classy and sophisticated I am, you're going to love my strongest recollection about the morning of my wedding: I thought I was going to shit my dress.

You see, I suffer from a nervous affliction that kicks in whenever I have something important on. I believe the technical term for it is 'squirty-bum'. For example, I've always had squirty-bum before a stand-up gig. And I don't mean an hour or so before I go on stage, I mean for the whole day. Stand-up gigs generally happen at night, right? My squirty-bum kicks in from whenever I wake up in the morning (usually around seven, when The Bloke gets up to get ready for work and I get up to watch him get ready for work) and carries on intermittently throughout the day, right up until I arrive at the venue. It's a steady and thorough process of elimination that no amount of Imodium has ever been able to control.

I've always thought of this phenomenon as my body's way of gradually bailing on me in the lead-up to any important event. With each visit to the smallest room of the house I imagine tiny voices going 'See ya!' and 'Hope it all goes well!' as they exit my internal workings and move on to greener (or is that browner?) pastures. Not that this bothers or upsets me in any way. Rather, it's a real celebration. You see, the Psiakis family suffers from a curse, and that curse is constipation (hey – now we're really getting to know each other!).

For years my paternal lineage has been tormented by the curse. You've heard of the Great Depression – well, my family lives through the Great Obstruction on a daily basis. Wait – what am I saying? The thought of anything happening for us on a daily basis is just ridiculous.

I think this explains why I always enjoy a good poo story. You know how you'll be out somewhere and occasionally someone might tell a story involving poo? Most people freak out or get angry, saying things like 'That's disgusting!' and 'Do you really think that's suitable subject matter for the dinner table during a chocolate mousse dessert?' Not me. I love a good poo story. Not in a weird fetish kind of way. I'm just very open when it comes to poo. Well, technically I guess I'm closed but I'm open to talking about it and so is the rest of my family. One of my sisters once rang me and when I asked, 'How are you?' she answered, 'I had the best poo today' and not only was I not in the least bit surprised by her answer but I also understood exactly what she meant and responded with 'Hooray!'

Whatever.

So, anyway, while squirty-bum is usually a welcome addition to my life due to the fact that it provides a temporary reprieve from the family curse, it brought a great deal of stress to me on my wedding day. Because the other deal with me is that when I have to go, I get one warning and then that's it. So every time I had a 'knock at the door' (so to speak) on the morning of my wedding, I pretty much dropped whatever I was doing and ran. You don't want to shit yourself on your wedding day. It's not a good look at the best of times but what a downer on the most important day of your life. It's the reason why I delayed actually putting on my wedding dress for as long as I possibly could. Could you imagine if I'd shat my dress? Who walks down the aisle with a jumper tied around their waist?

Apart from all the squirt-based shenanigans, the lead-up to departure for the ceremony was actually quite pleasant and remarkably calm. I didn't feel any anxiety about getting married – all I felt was excitement (and some distinct clenching sensations). My parents, bridesmaids, grandma and some other family members were all there. We drank champagne while we had our hair and make-up done and we made sure we had a bite to eat. In a stroke of wog genius, my mum had made a huge tray of spinach and ricotta lasagna the previous night. One by one, as everyone got hungry we reheated a piece so that nobody left the house with an empty stomach, which was important considering that there was alcohol on the horizon but a full meal was still hours away. The lasagna really was a great idea: everyone served themselves so Mum didn't have to worry about looking after people and it was the perfect thing to eat because it was light but still filling. Clever Mum.

Sadly, however, that lasagna also brought about the only moment of the day when I nearly cracked it. Picture this: the wedding cars had arrived and I was ready to set off for the ceremony. The only thing stopping me was the fact that my grandmother and one of my aunties were in the kitchen, still wearing aprons, arguing over whether it was okay to store the leftover lasagna in the oven or whether it should be glad-wrapped and placed in the fridge. It was a punctual arrival at the ceremony versus a world of salmonella and I still believe I was well within my rights to yell, 'Get those fucking aprons off and get in the fucking car!' There's nothing like a bride in a couture gown standing outside her family home, using every expletive under the sun and directing it all towards members of her own family. It was like *Cinderella* meets *Sylvania Waters*. And the videographer got it all on tape.

WHAT CAN I DO TO MAKE SURE EVERYTHING GOES TO PLAN AND I STAY CALM BEFORE I LEAVE FOR THE CEREMONY?

Before I give you some tips, know this: sometimes, even with all the planning and organising in the world, things don't go exactly to plan. It will not be the end of the world if your hairdresser calls to say they're stuck in traffic and they're going to be late. Everything will be all right. Repeat, everything will be all right. Now pour yourself a stiff one and check out my top tips for doing what you can:

- Have a schedule or running order and put one of your bridesmaids in charge of getting everyone to stick to it. This will go a long way towards keeping everyone and everything organised, minimising the need for panic. Draw up the schedule a day or so before the wedding and include things like your wake-up, breakfast and bathing times, arrival times for hair and make-up artists (or appointment times if you're doing this in a salon), times for everyone to have their hair and make-up done if that's happening at home (check with your hair and make-up artists because they'll have the best idea of the timeframes you should allow), dressing times for everyone, arrival time for your flowers if they're being delivered (or pick-up times if someone's going to get them), arrival time for the photographer, time for family and bridal party photos before you leave, arrival time for your transport and finally, departure time.

- Allow a little extra time for your bathing. It's the only time you'll have all day to be alone with your thoughts so make the most of it! Have a bath, use luxurious products – after all the rushing, planning, organising and checking, this is your starting point to relax and enjoy the actuality of getting married. (Yes, I said 'actuality'. I did Arts at uni.)

- Allow an extra 45 minutes to an hour on the end of your schedule. Trust me – if the flowers arrive late, or you have make-up issues or it takes longer than you thought to get dressed, this extra time will disappear. And if none of that happens and everything goes according to your schedule, you'll have time to relax with your family, get some extra photos or do some last minute touch-ups before you leave.

- Have the contact numbers of make-up artists, hairdressers, florists, transport providers etc. all printed clearly somewhere on your schedule so that the bridesmaid in charge of the schedule can call them immediately if they're late.

- I know you never thought you'd hear me say this but don't drink too much alcohol before you go. A little bit of champagne will steady your nerves and get you in the mood to celebrate but too much and you'll be slurring your vows (almost as classy as shitting your dress).

- Don't let your hairdresser or make-up artist leave until you're completely happy with their work. Letting them go and then trying to do your own salvage work if you don't like something always ends in tears.

- If you're making final payments on delivery/ completion of services, have them all ready. I had envelopes of cash clearly labeled for my hairdresser, make-up artist and florist so that when the time came to pay them on the day, all I had to do was hand over an envelope instead of rummage through my purse or dick around with cheques.

- Lay all your clothes out the day before, right down to your jewellery, shoes and underwear. That way you know you've got everything in the one place and there'll be no rushing around trying to find things when you're getting dressed.

- If you're wearing hosiery of any kind, consider wearing cotton gloves while you're putting your stockings on to eliminate the chances of putting ladders in them.

- Try not to eat, drink or smoke after you've put on your gown to avoid staining it (water is okay but still be careful).
- Try not to allow pets, accident-prone kids or spewy babies near you after you've put on your gown.
- Ask a bridesmaid to put an Emergency Bag into the car that's taking you to the ceremony and make sure that same bridesmaid ensures the Emergency Bag travels with you to the reception.

WHAT'S AN EMERGENCY BAG?

As the name suggests, it's a bag containing a bunch of stuff you'll need in case of emergency. You could include any of the following:

- Touch-up make-up, including the lipstick you're wearing
- Eye drops
- Spare contact lenses
- A brush/comb
- Extra bobby pins
- Hairspray
- Tissues/handkerchiefs
- Tampons (God forbid!)
- Asthma inhaler or antihistamines if you use them, and any other medication you take over the course of a day

- Deodorant
- Perfume
- Bach Rescue Remedy – a natural anti-stress remedy
- Aspirin
- Breath mints
- Nail file
- Bottle of the nail colour you're wearing
- Clear nail polish to dab onto hosiery runs
- Spare hosiery just in case
- Copies of your wedding speech and your Almost-Husband's wedding speech
- Tweezers
- Safety pins – including a couple of big ones in case something really fucks up
- Mini sewing-kit with scissors
- Bandaids
- Toothbrush, toothpaste, floss
- Piece of chalk (depending on your dress fabric, chalk can cover dark smears or stains on your dress)
- Hem or sticky tape, or Hollywood tape
- Spare earring backs
- Small tube of glue (if you have jewels or crystals on your shoes, gown or accessories)
- Bottle of water.

Your Emergency Bag is probably more of a medium-sized tote than a dainty clutch purse! And in the interests of balance, you probably don't need any of these in your Emergency Bag:

- Glock 9mm semi-automatic pistol
- 1987 Yellow Pages A–K
- Chipolatas
- Angle grinder
- Your vibrator (or anyone else's, for that matter)
- Bottle of hydrochloric acid
- Whoopee cushion
- Washing-up gloves
- TV guide
- Flea collar
- Netball trophy
- Postage stamps
- Recipe for Anzac biscuits
- Wireless router
- Footy fixture
- Hand grenade
- Gardening secateurs
- Gladwrap
- Moth balls
- Assorted padlocks.

BLOKE'S WORLD

On the day

Being nervous or emotional on the day of your wedding is totally normal and okay. Being hungover is not. By all means have a beer or two if you want to the night before but your aim should be to wake up refreshed and well-rested, not nauseous and throwing up into your cornflakes.

Similarly, don't get tanked before the ceremony, and make sure you and your groomsmen have something to eat before you leave for the wedding. This is a great excuse to get your mum to make you the biggest cooked breakfast in the world. If you're getting ready from the venue, a hotel or anywhere else that's not your house or your parents' place, plan ahead as far as food goes. We had an afternoon service and The Bloke and his groomsmen got ready from our venue. He asked his mum to bring them pile of fresh-baked rolls and ham off the bone so they could knock back a champion lunch with a couple of Crownies to take the edge off both their hunger and their nerves, and it saved their bellies from rumbling during the ceremony.

Consider drawing up a schedule or running order for what has to happen before you leave for the ceremony and put your best man in charge of seeing that everyone sticks to it. It might sound extreme but it will go a long way towards ensuring your preparations run smoothly. Include things like breakfast, dressing time, arrival/pick up times for buttonhole flowers, arrival time for the photographer, arrival time for your transport and departure time. Have contact numbers for the photographer, florist and transport clearly marked on the schedule so you can call them directly if you need to without having to trouble (or panic) your Nearly-Wife.

Lay your clothes out the night before, right down to your underwear and accessories so you're not rushing around trying to find things when you get dressed. Your aim should be to keep your preparations as relaxed and easy as possible, and while laying out your clothes may be reminiscent of your first day of primary school, it can help.

If you're not at your parents' place, consider having a mini sewing-kit (and someone who knows how to use one) on hand in the event of buttons coming off shirts because it happens.

Take extra care when you're shaving so you don't rock up to the ceremony looking like a cross between Norman Gunston and Freddy Krueger.

Make sure your best man is on top of the wedding ring situation. Nominate another person to check that he has them with him when you all leave for the ceremony in case you forget or your best man forgets (a perfect job for one of your parents). You and your best man might also like to entrust a copy of your speeches to this person for them to slip into a jacket pocket or handbag.

Your preparations won't take anywhere near as long as your Nearly-Wife's because you won't have to worry about hair and make-up artists for you or groomsmen (unless you're all outrageously metrosexual). If you're having an afternoon ceremony, consider spending your morning doing something other than sitting on the couch and scratching yourself: a hit of golf, a massage (not that kind of massage) a swim, a ride or a long walk with the dog are all great ways to chill out and you can also involve your groomsmen or even your dad for some last-minute pre-wedding secret men's business. The Bloke told me that in hindsight, he would have loved to spend the morning of our wedding at the TAB. I'm secretly glad he didn't. I don't know what I would have done if he'd asked to have the calls of the races he bet on piped into the reception.

Your Nearly-Wife's preparations will be quite involved and there's every chance she might be a little stressed about them on the day. Having a small gift, some flowers or simply just a handwritten note delivered to her while she's getting ready will totally make her day and guarantee she brags about you to anyone who'll listen for ages afterwards. The gift doesn't have to be expensive and the flowers could be as simple as a single stem, and you could arrange for someone from your crew to deliver them to her. At the very least, give her a call. If tensions are running high in Bridetown she'll appreciate a few calming words to bring her focus back to what the day's about: the two of you (and unlimited drinks at the reception).

SoMEThInG oLD, NEW, BoRRoweD AND BLUE

Wearing something old, something new, something borrowed and something blue is a wedding tradition dating back to the Victorian era that's still observed by many brides today.

The tradition is meant to bring good luck to the bride in four ways: something old is meant to symbolise a link between the bride, her family and the past. Something new represents optimism for the new life ahead of her. Something borrowed symbolises the 'rubbing off' of the good fortune of a happily married friend or family member and the fact that the bride will always have friends or family to rely on. And something blue represents modesty, purity and fidelity, as symbolised by this colour since ancient times. (You know how the Virgin Mary's always dressed in blue when you see her? When you see pictures of her, that is – if you're actually catching up with her for coffee we probably need you to lie down for a while.)

On my wedding day I wore a bunch of stuff that covered all the old, new, borrowed and blue bases. My grandmother's wedding ring, which she gave me to wear pinned to the inside of my dress, was my official 'something old' as well as 'something borrowed'. My 'something new' was my dress, my shoes and my knickers. My official 'something borrowed' was my mum's veil and her earrings. And the garter The Bloke's grandmother wore on her wedding day was my official 'something blue' as well as 'something borrowed'. As you can see, I like to go over and above the call.

Because of my Greek heritage, I also observed a bunch of other traditions and superstitions. Firstly, here's the deal with me and superstitions: I don't really believe in them, but because I'm a pessimist I observe them all. For example, when I bought my first car my grandmother threw a handful of rice into it for luck (it's a wog thing). Because I'm addicted to cleaning (also, I suspect, a wog thing), I picked up every single grain. But because I'm a pessimist, instead of throwing the grains out I put them neatly in the glove box – it'll be just my luck that the day I throw them out, I'll crash the car.

That's just how I think, and I can't help it. The worst bit is that I'm imposing the way I think onto The Bloke. And worse still, he's letting me. For example, I make sure we don't ever hand a knife directly to each other: I put the knife down for The Bloke to pick up or he puts the knife down for me to pick up. The reason for that is because there's a Greek superstition that says that if two people ever have their hands on the same knife at the same time, they'll come to blows. Which The Bloke thought was quite the prospect until I explained that 'come to blows' actually means 'have a fight'.

In any case, for my wedding, Wog Rules decreed that I had to spend the night before the big day under my parents' roof. On the day, just before we left for the wedding ceremony, I had to do a couple of things involving thresholds, which are symbolic of moving from one life into another. First I had to dip the index finger of my right hand into a jar of honey and paint a small cross above the open door. This is to symbolise the beginning of a life that would be sweet and blessed. After that my mum put a small glass of water on the threshold and I had to knock it over with a backwards kick into the house on my way out. This is meant to represent washing away my 'old' life in readiness to start a new one. I can honestly tell you that if the

NapiSan Man had turned up while all that was going on I don't know what he would have thought.

Aside from my grandmother's wedding ring, I also had a pair of little scissors and an evil eye talisman pinned to the inside of my dress. The scissors were to cut wagging tongues (symbolically, not literally – I doubt nail scissors from the $2 shop would do much damage), and the evil eye talisman was a blue glass bead in the shape of an eye that would protect me against anyone who would look upon me with hatred or malice (not that I remember inviting any of those people to the wedding). Seriously, there were so many secret things going on beneath my dress it was like ASIO under there.

Not even brides are safe from knick-knockers.

THE BRIDAL POSSE

Traditionally, a bride was attended only by bridesmaids and a groom only by groomsmen. While this is still the case for many bridal couples, it's not the only option. In fact, I'd even go so far as to say that the hard and fast rules of who attends whom went out with puffy-sleeved taffeta bridesmaid's dresses and Loony Tunes novelty ties for groomsmen (and yes, they're definitely out – I checked).

I'm lucky enough to have a bunch of extremely close female friends who I grew up with and love dearly but my all-time bestest friend has testicles and we'd always joked that if I ever got married he'd be my maid of honour. When the time came for The Bloke and I to decide who we'd be attended by at our wedding, I came up with my two sisters and my best mate and The Bloke came up with his brother, his sister and his best mate. So with a total of three girls and three guys, we decided that I'd have three bridesmaids and The Bloke would have three groomsmen. We also chose The Bloke's cousin and two of my cousins as our two pageboys and flower girl because we adore them and really wanted kids in our wedding party (especially me – I believe it's auspicious. And yes, that's probably a wog thing).

When it came to groomsmen and bridesmaids, we put the girls on my side and the guys on The Bloke's side only because we thought it would look better when we were all standing in a row during the ceremony. However, where they stood didn't strictly define who they were standing for. (Although The Bloke and my best mate are firm friends and I consider The Bloke's sister the big sister I never had.) I've also been to weddings where the bride has been attended by one or more 'bridesboys' and the groom has been attended by one or more 'groomsgirls'. Another wedding I went to saw the bride attended only by a 'man of honour' and the groom attended by a 'best woman'. Basically, the rule of having women attend a bride and men attend a groom no longer applies. Nowadays you can have pretty much whoever you choose in your bridal posse and give them the title you think best suits their role. Just be mindful of the impression that the title of 'bridesmole' will give on your order of service and don't ask me what you'd call a transgender cross-dressing lesbian standing for the groom. (Tracey?)

How Many Attendants Should I Have?

The number of attendants you choose to have depends on a number of factors. If you're only having 50 guests to your wedding, you'll look ridiculous with 17 bridesmaids. If you're footing the bill for everything bridesmaid-related and your Almost-Husband is paying for everything groomsmen-related this could also influence how many attendants you have, as will the number of siblings and/or special family members you'd like to include.

Once you know how large or small your wedding is going to be, this will give you a starting point for how many attendants you should choose. A small, intimate wedding usually lends itself to fewer attendants whereas if you're having a big, lavish celebration you can go large if you want to. These rules aren't set in stone – ultimately you should choose your attendants based on the people who are closest to you and who you think will be the best people to have around you in the lead-up to the wedding as well as on the day. Just bear in mind that the more bridesmaids you have, the more people you have to get to agree on things like outfits, shoes, hairstyles and all that crap.

Also, regardless of how many attendants you choose to have, never underestimate the impact of a bridesmaid who looks hot to trot. I've heard some people joke that you shouldn't choose anyone who's likely to steal your thunder in the hot-diggity stakes but I beg to differ. It doesn't matter if it's raining, the food's shit and the DJ's just played something by Celine Dion: nothing perks up a wedding like a bunch of bridesmaids who are hot as balls. Why do you think they get toasted so often during the speeches?

I'VE CHOSEN MY BRIDESMAIDS. THEY'RE HOT. NOW WHAT?

If you haven't already chosen your dress, do so and then start looking for your bridesmaids' outfits. There are a number of ways to go about bridesmaid's dress shopping. Some (brave) brides take all their bridesmaids out shopping together to find something they all like, whether it be an off-the-rack purchase or a style that they're going to have made by a dressmaker. Other brides take only their maid or matron of honour to select a shortlist of dresses and then take the other bridesmaids along and try to get everyone to agree on something from the shortlist. And some brides do all the shortlisting and even all the choosing themselves and expect their bridesmaids to go with the flow. Finding something that makes everyone happy isn't always easy, particularly if you're dealing with different body types and body image issues, different personalities and expectations when it comes to who's paying for what and what's considered financially reasonable.

I explained to my bridesmaids that my main priority was for their dresses to be an off-the-rack style that would complement mine and a style that would be easy for them to wear because I didn't want them feeling stressed or uncomfortable on the day. Since my bridesmaids and I had decided that they would pay for their dresses I also wanted them to be the sort of outfits they'd be able to wear again after the wedding, say to a classy party or formal function. A tall order, but I had hope.

Because The Bloke's sister lives in Western Australia and I'm a Melbourne girl, I took my two sisters shopping to Chadstone Shopping Centre. (Being one of the most easygoing people I've ever met, The Bloke's sister was fine with not being there and said she didn't give a flying continental what we chose as long as – and I quote – 'it doesn't have poofy sleeves or make a rustling noise when I walk.') The idea was that I'd give my sisters an idea of the sorts of styles I liked and thought were suitable, but because their fashion knowledge and interest far outweighed mine I was more than open to suggestions. And – importantly – I promised I wouldn't make them wear anything they hated with a passion.

Because I was keen for them to be able to wear their outfits again after the wedding, we stayed away from shops that specifically sold bridesmaid dresses, mainly because they all tended to be a bit formal and some were just downright feral. (Tip: a bridesmaid's dress should never look like something Barbie would wear.) My sisters and I looked at a whole lot of women's stores that stocked cocktail dresses and any other outfits suitable for wearing 'after five'. The major upmarket department stores were our starting point because they stocked a range of labels – we found a few labels we liked and then checked out their stores in the mall to see their full range. I showed my sisters the sorts of colours I liked (latte, antique roses and creams) and explained that I preferred a classic style to something modern, then basically just let them loose to find outfits they liked.

About six hours later we decided on strapless sheath dresses from Review. They were dark ivory with an antique rose lace detail over the bust and a satin, latte-coloured belt. We didn't like the latte satin around the waist because we thought it chopped the body in half so after purchasing the dresses we had them altered so that the satin belt sat right under the bust, giving the dresses an instant empire-line that mirrored the empire-line on my dress. The alteration cost about $15 per dress, bringing the total cost of each dress to $265. Given that they had chosen dresses they could definitely wear again after the wedding, we were all really happy with this price.

My bridesmaids were all content to wear the same dress but your bridesmaids don't have to. My crew all had very similar heights and builds so the style looked great on all of them, but if you're dealing with hugely different body shapes you might consider having them wear the same colour but in different styles. (You might choose to have their dresses made if you're doing this so they can all be cut from the same fabric.) You can also dress them in the same style but different colours to suit your desired colour scheme. There's no rule that says bridesmaids must be dressed identically: I've been to a wedding where the maid of honour wore a dress that was different to the other bridesmaids' dresses, and another wedding where all the bridesmaids were dressed completely differently to each other. (They all looked stunning but knowing how hard it is to find one perfect bridesmaid's dress, I can only imagine how hard it must have been to find four!)

HINTS FOR BRIDESMAID'S OUTFIT SHOPPING

- Before you even begin shopping, find out if there's anything your bridesmaids really don't feel comfortable wearing. For example, some people don't like strapless styles, plunging necklines or short hemlines. Of course you want your bridesmaids to look fantastic, but I can guarantee you they want to feel that way, too. Dressing them in styles they're comfortable in will also ensure they have all the time in the world to attend to you, as opposed to spending half the day fussing over themselves in the bathroom or hiding behind trees when it's time for photos.

- If your bridesmaids won't all be in the same outfit, make sure that the outfits you choose complement each other. Choosing a 'theme' (such as a particular dress feature, neckline, skirt shape, etc.) can help achieve this.

- If you're having your bridesmaids' dresses made and they're all wearing the same colour, ensure that all the fabric you buy is from the same dye lot to eliminate the chance of colour discrepancies.

- The bridesmaids' outfits shouldn't just be stunning on their own, they should also be stunning in the way they complement your wedding gown. I took a picture of my dress with me so that when my sisters and I found a bridesmaids' dress we liked we could see what it looked like next to mine. Try to match classic outfits to a classic gown, modern outfits to a modern gown, etc. Again, consider choosing a 'theme' to tie the bridesmaids' outfits to yours.

- When it comes to shoes, be as considerate towards your bridesmaids' feet as you are towards your own. Skyscraper heels could mean the end of a friendship, or at the very least an ensemble cast of bridesmaid death-stares in your direction by the end of the night. And don't forget to have your bridesmaids break in their shoes, too.

- Allow plenty of time if the bridesmaids' outfits need alterations. Book the alteration appointments in advance so can get all your bridesmaids there at once and the dressmaker has enough time to spend with you. Depending on the alterations required you might need to have shoes and bras organised in time for the appointment, too (to make sure the dressmaker gets hemlines, necklines and seams right).

- Consider having your bridesmaids' dresses dry-cleaned before the big day. Regardless of whether they've been purchased off-the-rack or made, they can get marked through handling and trying-on. (This can also happen when they're being altered.) Having them dry-cleaned and kept in garment bags until the day of the wedding ensures you don't have to worry about the unpleasant discovery of marks or stains when it's too late to do anything about them.

- If you're marrying during the cooler months and you're having outdoor photos, consider buying your bridesmaids a pashmina or simple wrap to wear. Outdoor photos often involve the bridal party doing a lot of standing around and waiting and if the weather's cold you don't want your bridesmaids turning blue (unless that's the look you're going for in your photos). If you're having your bridesmaids' dresses made an easy option is to buy some extra fabric for your dressmaker to make matching wraps from.

- When it comes to flower girls, pay particular attention to dress length. Little kids can struggle to walk with long hemlines and you don't want them continually stepping on and dirtying the front of their dress or worse, falling over. If you have your heart set on them wearing a full-length dress, ensure the hemline finishes a couple of inches from the ground.

Who Pays for what when it comes to The bridesmaids' outfits?

Once upon a time the bride's parents paid for everything, including everything required for the bridal party. As generous as they are, I think that if I'd asked my parents to pay for everything they would have laughed in my face and then started crying hysterically.

My bridesmaids paid for their own dresses. I paid for their shoes and accessories and my mum shouted their professional hair and make-up costs on the day of the wedding. (What a star.) We didn't agree on a price limit for their outfits beforehand because we had no idea what things would cost but one of my sisters later told me she'd expected to pay about $300. If you want to be ultra-fair you could consider going halves on everything with your bridesmaids but general practice nowadays seems to be for the bridesmaids to pay for their dresses and the bride to pay for everything else. Everybody's budget is different, though, and the best advice I can give you is to be upfront – discuss with your bridesmaids what you all think is reasonable in terms of cost (and the best time to do this is *before* you go shopping).

When it came to our flower girl and pageboys, The Bloke and I had agreed that we would pay for their outfits as our gift to them for being part of our wedding. We didn't want to dress them in formal attire because we felt that little kids should be free to be just that, and putting them in stuffy clothes would probably make them feel uncomfortable and could possibly freak them out. (Could you imagine someone trying to make you wear a bow-tie at age four?) Since each child would be walking down the aisle next to a bridesmaid, we wanted their outfits to complement what the bridesmaids were wearing, so we shopped around at a few children's clothing stores and found little pinstriped pants and vest sets with an ivory shirt for our pageboys and an ivory party-dress with an empire-line bow for our flower girl. The only thing we asked the kids' parents to purchase for them was their shoes, because kids' footwear can be tricky and we wanted to make sure the kids ended up with the right shoes for their feet. We also thought that the shoes would probably be the part of the outfit that the kids would be most likely to get continued wear from after the wedding, so better for their parents to make the selection – we just specified the colours we were after.

What Should I Expect My Maid/Matron of Honour And My Bridesmaids To Actually Do?

The maid/matron of honour (maid if she's unmarried, matron if she's already hitched) is usually the bride's closest friend or relative and traditionally performs the following duties:

- Organises the bridal shower and hens' night (if you're having them)
- Coordinates bridesmaids' activities before the wedding (e.g. dress fittings) and on the day (e.g. getting ready)

- Is the main assistant to you before the wedding for everything from shopping for bridal wear to helping with invitations and wedding favours
- Helps you get dressed on the big day
- Makes sure you have something to eat at some stage before you leave for the ceremony
- Signs the marriage certificate during the ceremony as an official witness
- Holds your bouquet during the ceremony
- Arranges your veil and the train of your dress during the ceremony and photographs
- Makes a speech at the reception
- Dances with the best man at the reception
- Brings gifts to your house or your parents' house after the wedding
- Holds your hair back when you spew (this last one may not apply, depending on how classy you are).

Apart from looking hot at all times, bridesmaids also have a number of traditional duties and responsibilities. These include:

- Being available for dress fittings and shopping expeditions
- Helping to make the wedding favours
- Assembling a wedding day emergency kit (see What's An Emergency Bag, page 187) and keeping it somewhere safe in case it's needed

- Kid-wrangling with regard to pageboys and flower girls
- Ensuring that the wedding guest book (if there is one) makes its way around to all the guests at the reception and is collected afterwards
- Assisting you in any way as requested either by you or your maid/matron of honour
- Dancing with the groomsmen at the reception
- Holding the skirt of your wedding gown up and out of harm's way when you go to the toilet. I'm serious.

All the above duties are just traditional guidelines – you can organise your attendants pretty much any way you please. Bridesmaids can help with the maid/matron of honour's duties and sometimes a bride might even choose to do them on her own. For example, The Bloke and I organised our own hens' and bucks' activities (see page 135) and gave the task of signing the marriage certificate to our grandmothers. To keep things simple, you can delegate specific tasks among your attendants and just make sure they're all aware of the general stuff.

In the interests of balance, here's a list of activities that your maid/matron of honour and bridesmaids should not perform:

- Cracking onto your Almost-Husband
- Cracking onto your dad

- Cracking onto the priest or celebrant (at least, not during your ceremony – what they do in their own time is up to them)
- Exposing themselves, either intentionally or unintentionally, to your guests
- Requesting that your DJ play Kevin Bloody Wilson's 'I Knew The Bride When She Used To Be A Moll'
- Pulling bongs in the carpark (they should only do this in the bridal lounge).

WHAT DO FLOWER GIRLS AND PAGEBOYS ACTUALLY DO?

The duties and responsibilities of flower girls and pageboys should be kept to a minimum – after all, they're just kids. Traditionally, pageboys (who can also be known as ring-bearers, but then again, aren't we all?) are the first to walk down the aisle during the ceremony while carrying a fancy pillow with the bride and groom's wedding rings attached. Often the rings aren't actually the real rings but just 'symbolic' rings, with the best man in charge of the real ones for safe keeping. Flower girls traditionally follow the maid/matron of honour and bridesmaids down the aisle, scattering rose petals along the way to prepare for the bride's entrance.

However, it's important to note that it doesn't always work out this way – even with all the coaxing and rehearsals in the world, kids can be unpredictable and might still refuse to carry out these duties. If you're worried or just want to make the whole thing a little less scary for your young attendants, do what The Bloke and I did and have your flower girls or pageboys be escorted down the aisle by a bridesmaid who can hold their hand and hopefully prevent them from freaking out and soiling themselves (not necessarily in that order).

BLOKE'S WORLD

The bridal posse

Before we go any further, let me just say this: do not crack onto any of the bridesmaids. Even as a joke. They're going to look hot but Just. Don't. Crack. Onto. Any. Bridesmaids.

Righty-o, then. As far as dressing your groomsmen goes, it's covered in BLOKE'S WORLD – Suit Yourself (page 83). So let's have a squiz at what your crew are actually meant to do for you.

Traditionally, your best man is your closest friend or relative and they're meant to cover the following duties and responsibilities:

- Organising the bucks' night (if you're having one)
- Coordinating fittings for the groomsmen's suits and shirts

- Helping you choose ties and accessories
- Helping you organise wedding transport for your Nearly-Wife and her bridal posse as well as for you and your crew. (The fancy cars are usually used to transport the bride, bride's parents and bridesmaids – you might consider a separate hire car to get you and your groomsmen to the ceremony. Don't rely on a taxi. Your best man might drive if he's not drinking until the reception and he's happy to leave his car there overnight.)
- Helping you get dressed on the big day
- Making sure you have something to eat before you leave for the ceremony
- Being your right-hand man on the day, there to assist you with whatever you need
- Keeping the wedding rings safe until the exchange of rings during the ceremony
- Signing the marriage certificate during the ceremony as an official witness
- Making a speech at the reception
- Dancing with the maid/matron of honour at the reception
- Returning any hired formalwear after the wedding
- Bringing gifts to your place or your parents' place after the wedding
- Making sure your Nearly-Wife never, ever finds out about that stripper.

Your groomsmen's duties include:

- Being available for suit fittings, shirt fittings and any other shopping expeditions

- Helping organise the bucks' night
- Assisting you in any way before or during the wedding, as requested by you or the best man
- Helping the bridesmaids wrangle any pageboys or flower girls
- Dancing with the bridesmaids at the reception
- Letting you know if your fly's undone at any stage during the wedding.

And, in the interests of balance, here's a list of activities your best man and groomsmen should not perform:

- Cracking onto your Nearly-Wife
- Cracking onto your mum
- Cracking onto your nan (unless she's really gagging for it)
- Putting Rohypnol in the drink of anyone at the wedding
- Lighting farts at any stage during the celebrations
- Loudly rating the bridesmaids' racks (although, let's face it, they're all going to look awesome).

THE
PHOTOGRAPHER

I left booking a photographer until towards the end of the planning process because I thought it was simply a matter of calling someone up and booking them in. The truth of the matter? Hahahahahahaha.

Booking a good photographer who won't charge you the earth actually requires a bit of research and legwork. Firstly, decide what sort of photos you'd like. If you're like The Bloke and your decision is simply 'Um . . . wedding photos?' think again, because there are many different types of wedding photos. Do you want highly stylised shots that look like they've come straight out of a glamour magazine? Or would you prefer natural, candid shots? Do you want your photos to look arty and designed or would you rather that they just capture a moment, as though the subjects weren't even aware they were having their photo taken? Do you want formal, casual, romantic or funny shots? Do you want colour shots? Black and white? Sepia? Hand-coloured photos? And what sort of album do you want: traditional matte-cut photos or a more modern, printed design?

The best way to decide on your answers to these questions is to research a few wedding photographers. If you have friends whose wedding photos you've seen and you really like, find out who their photographer was. Most wedding photographers provide comprehensive websites that will not only show you the sorts of photos they take but will also give you an idea of their fees and the packages that are available. For example, a photographer will charge varying rates depending on how long you require their services. The photographer The Bloke and I used took photos at my house before the ceremony, at the venue where The Bloke and his groomsmen were getting ready, during the ceremony, in the gardens after the ceremony, and during the first part of our reception. Other people choose to have their photographer present for the entire night – it all depends on your budget and the kinds of photos you want taken.

When you know what sort of photos you're after and the price range you're looking at, narrow your choice down to a few photographers and then make an appointment to visit them. This is a really important part of the process. It's a good idea to meet the photographer and see if you like them. This is the person who's going to be asking you to look at them and smile all day. If you discover too late that this person is a rude/bossy/arrogant/daggy/impatient/ mildly crazed arsehole, you're likely to find it harder to smile when they ask you to. The fact is that it's just easier to smile at someone you genuinely like.

Visiting a few photographers also enables you to ask them some very important questions, such as:

- *What exactly is included in your total price?* This will determine how much bang you're going to get for your buck and help you figure out what – if any – extra costs are involved.
- *Can you suggest locations or shots that will complement our wedding style?* You don't have to just have photos in and around your venue(s). Depending on how much time you plan on allowing for photos, a good photographer will be able to suggest heaps of photo locations that will suit your style (bearing in mind that the further you have to travel, the more time it will take and the more it may cost, especially if your photographer charges travel fees). Cafés, interesting or iconic buildings, old bridges, city laneways, beach boxes,

amusement parks, trams, aquariums, grand hotel foyers or ballrooms – the possibilities are limited only by your photographer's imagination.

- *Have you taken photos at our ceremony/reception venue before?* If they have, they'll be familiar with your venue and will be likely to know all the best spots for photos. This is particularly important if your venue has extensive grounds – you want a photographer who's going to take you straight to all the best photo locations instead of wasting your time by leading you from one clearing to another in an effort to find the best spot (which also wastes your money, as most photographers charge by the hour). If your photographer has worked at your venue before you should definitely ask to see some of the photos – you may see some shots/locations you'd like to use for your day.

- *If you have taken photos at our venue(s) before, what's your bad weather contingency plan?* If your photographer is familiar with your venue they'll know the best place to go if the weather's not conducive to outdoor photos. For example, one of my friends had a photographer who saved the (rainy) day by taking the bridal party to a little park near their venue with an outdoor pavilion that was perfect for photos, enabling them to still have 'garden' shots undercover.

- *If you have taken photos at our venue(s) before, are there any light requirements we should know about?* This sounds like an odd question but trust me, it could save your photos. On the advice of our photographer we changed our ceremony time so that it would start an hour earlier after she explained that the light at the end of the day starts to disappear earlier on Mount Dandenong than it does elsewhere, and if the light wasn't good our outdoor photos wouldn't be either. Genius.

- *Will ours be the only booking you take on our wedding day?* My strong advice to you is not to book a photographer who has any other booking on the day of your wedding. Don't risk them either being late or rushing you so they can get to their next job.

- *How will we be able to view the photos after the wedding day?* Our photographer gave us a boxful of standard-sized proofs to look through and keep. When it came time to choose the shots for our album, we also went to visit her and she showed us every shot on her big flat-screen TV (like a slide show) to narrow down a shortlist and then make a final selection. A week or so later we went back to watch her TV again, this time to see how she had arranged all the album pages and suggest any changes. Different photographers work differently, so make sure you establish your viewing options up-front.

- *Do you retain ownership of all our images or are we able to purchase them from you?* Most photographers will lock you in to purchase a wedding album or selected number of prints before they give you the opportunity to buy all your images from them. This is fairly standard and part of their business. However, once you've committed to the album or prints you want a photographer who'll sell your images to you for a reasonable fee so that if you want to make copies of photos for friends, relatives, etc., you can do it yourself rather than be running to (and paying) your photographer. And if you purchase your images on a disk or CD, ensure it contains full-resolution images so that you can make different-sized copies (some photographers copy images onto disk or CD in such a way that if you want to make enlargements, you still have to go through them).

- *Will you be taking our photos on the day?* I've heard stories about couples meeting fabulous photographers who end up sending their assistant to take the wedding photos because they're 'ill' (read: doing another wedding elsewhere and maximising the earning capacity of a single day). Confirm that the person you're meeting with will be the same person who's actually going to take your photos and get it written into the contract if you feel any nagging doubts. Or better yet, find a photographer who makes you feel nothing but total confidence in them.

Something else you might like to consider when it comes to your wedding photos is giving your photographer a list of must-have shots before the wedding that they can have with them on the day. The list should contain all the shots you want (for example, photo with parents, photo with grandparents, photo with best friends from school, photo of the rings resting on the wedding certificate, big group photo of bridal party and guests, etc.) so that you don't have to try and remember every shot you want on the day and none of the shots you really want end up being forgotten.

Be very specific with your photographer about how long you want to spend taking photos. The Bloke and I didn't want to spend more than an hour taking photos while our guests had pre-dinner drinks because we wanted to be able to mingle with them at the tail-end of their drinks. If your photos go overtime and you're late to your reception, your reception may end up being rushed or if it in turn goes overtime, your venue may charge you a fee. And spare a thought for your guests, waiting for you to arrive while you're trying to get that one last shot.

Also be sure to let your photographer know if you want them to move around the reception and photograph your guests, and whether you want these photos to be posed or candid. The photographer The Bloke and I used took some brilliant shots of our guests while they didn't know their photos were being taken that we were able to send to them along with their thank-you cards as a special memento of the night.

Ask your photographer what else they can do with your photos apart from put them in an album. Some photographers also do framing and photographic collages. The photographer who did my wedding designed and printed my thank-you cards. The Bloke and I chose one of her photos and the words we wanted printed on it and she put the whole thing together for us for a very reasonable fee. In fact, I loved the work she did on our wedding so much I used it in this book.

What say we blow this joint and hit the bar?

What About My Videographer?

My advice for your videographer is pretty much the same as my advice for your photographer – just substitute the word 'film' for the word 'photo'. Seriously.

THE TRANSPORT

I'm not into cars and neither is The Bloke so I can't say we went particularly ape-shit when it came to organising the transport for our wedding. In fact, we didn't even go so much as ape-fart. We just wanted something that wasn't a taxi or a relative or friend's car to get us where we needed to go.

The reason we didn't want a relative or friend's car was because we didn't want to burden them with the responsibility of driving it, but that's just a personal thing. I've heard of lots of couples who've called upon friends or relatives with classy wheels to drive them on their wedding day – it's particularly popular among grooms who just need someone to drive them and their groomsmen to the service (they usually get transported in the flashy bridal cars after that).

After deciding we wanted the most basic form of hire car with driver we figured out that what we'd be looking at would simply be either the latest model Ford or Holden sedan, so we rang around a few car hire companies to see who'd give us the best deal. Because The Bloke and his groomsmen were going to be getting ready from our venue and then staying on the mountain overnight, they were going to drive their cars up the mountain early on our wedding day and therefore wouldn't need hired transport of any kind.

I would be leaving from my parents' house and needed transport to take my parents, my bridesmaids and myself to the venue. (Our flower girl and pageboys were travelling with their parents.) The cars only had to drop us off at the venue and then leave – because we were having all our photos taken on-site and didn't have to travel anywhere else for them, there was no need for the cars to hang around. I didn't want a limousine or anything too over-the-top and because Dad's always been a Holden man, I decided to err on the side of being my father's daughter by settling on two Holden sedans to accommodate the six of us. We also needed transport to get The Bloke and me from our venue to our wedding night accommodation.

In the process of ringing around to get quotes I discovered two ridiculous things. Ridiculous thing number one: many car hire companies have a minimum call-out time and charge accordingly. For example, even though I only needed two cars for an hour each to get us to the ceremony, many of the companies I called provided a minimum two- or three-hour call-out with a minimum two- or three-hour price. It was a while before I found a company willing to do a one-hour call-out for a decent rate.

Ridiculous thing number two: our wedding night accommodation was about five minutes down the road from our wedding venue, meaning we needed a car for a five-minute drive. We weighed up our options: lift from a guest, taxi or hire car? Technically speaking, we also could have walked but neither of us thought that would be a particularly good look, especially if the weather turned out rotten. In the end, we eliminated getting a lift from a guest because a) there was a chance nobody at our wedding would be sober by the end of the night and b) we didn't want anyone else to know where we were staying. (We weren't keen to still be entertaining at 4 am!) We then eliminated a taxi because we thought it was probably a bit rich to ask a taxi driver to drive all the way up the mountain for a five-minute fare. We'd also recently heard a story about a newly-married couple who'd booked a taxi to take them from their reception to their wedding night venue and the taxi turned up late because the driver had been busy cleaning spew out of it. Nice. So we settled on getting one of our hire cars to return for us at an agreed time, and because we'd already given them our business on the day they didn't charge us the full rate for doing so. When I think about it, we still paid a ridiculous amount for a five-minute drive but at least the driver was sober, on time (in fact, he was early and happy to wait) and not draped in a fragrant cloud of Eau de Vom.

If you're looking for a task to delegate to your Almost-Husband, planning the wedding transport is perfect because let's face it: even if he's not mad for cars he's more likely to be interested in them than floral centrepieces. However, wedding transport isn't strictly a 'man's job' – in fact, I organised the transport for my wedding. The Bloke and I also recently heard a great story about a bride who not only organised transport for herself and her attendants but also surprised her Almost-Husband by organising for his all-time favourite hot-rod to get him and his groomsmen to the church on time. Regardless of who organises the transport, you can find some helpful suggestions over the following pages. And if you end up booking fancy cars so you can pose for photos near them, for God's sake keep your dress well away from the tyres. The tyre paint the operators use to give the wheels a glossy look can mark your dress, so beware.

BLOKE'S WORLD

The transport

Love cars? Awesome — here's the job for you. Couldn't give a flying continental about cars? That's okay too, but would you rather do this job or choose napkin rings? Thought so.

Organising your wedding transport can be a blast because you get to look at cool cars. However, before you get anywhere near a vehicle, there are a few details you'll need to lock down first:

- Where will you be getting ready for the ceremony? Also, where will your Nearly-Wife will be getting ready for the ceremony, and how many people need to be transported from each place? Is it just your Nearly-Wife and her bridesmaids or will her parents need transport as well?
- What time do you and your groomsmen need to be at the ceremony venue before the service starts and what time does your bride plan to arrive with her attendants? Work backwards from there and figure out what time you all need to be picked up.
- Can the cars leave after they've dropped you all off or do you need them to transport you to your photography location(s) and then to your reception?
- Do you need a car to return to your venue at the end of the reception to take you to your wedding night accommodation?

Once you know all these boring but very necessary details you can move on to the fun part of organising your wedding transport. (You need to know the above information first because these are the questions transport providers will ask you in order for them to give you an accurate quote.)

If there's a certain type of car you've got your heart set on, start investigating availability and costs. If you Google 'wedding car hire' in your area you'll find heaps of transport providers but if you're after something a little out of the ordinary (such as a rare type of car) you might find you have to do a more refined search to find exactly what you're after. Using the internet as a starting point is worthwhile because you'll get to see pictures of cars, which can help you decide on what you want. Actually viewing the cars in the person should happen when you've narrowed down your choices and you're ready to book.

Many car hire companies have websites that will calculate rough quotes for you but there'll be others that you'll have to ring. Getting at least four or five quotes is totally worth it because the price ranges vary according to the sort of car you're after. The industry is also very competitive – if you're a negotiator, here's a chance to use your skills to full advantage.

Choose cars that suit your wedding style – for example, vintage cars for a vintage-styled wedding, sleek sports cars for a more modern one. Just make sure there's room for a big dress and a veil and bear in mind that two-door cars that require passengers to squeeze themselves into the back seat like sardines probably aren't a great idea. Also bear in mind you don't have to opt for flashy cars if you don't want to, particularly if you're on a budget because the flashier the car, the more it's likely to cost you. Similarly, you can have friends or relatives with nice cars do the honours for transport as well, although if they have to take you from your reception to your wedding night accommodation you're basically asking them to abstain from drinking all night and this may not always be fair (or wise).

Some suggestions to help you organise your wedding transport include:

- Before locking in your booking, go and physically see the car(s) you're about to book. Photos on the net might show the car looking great on the outside but for all you know the interior's shot. Cracks or 'lifting' on leather seating can potentially damage certain dress fabrics and you'll never hear the end of it if your Nearly-Wife snags the back of her dress.
- If you're booking a limo, make sure your destinations (chapel, reception centre, etc.) have driveways big enough to accommodate the extra length.
- Take the time to talk to the transport providers and drivers you visit about your requirements. This will not only ensure you book someone who's able to meet your needs but will also give you a sense of what they're like – if they're a complete ball-breaker chances are you won't want them anywhere near you or your bridal party on the big day.
- When you make your booking times to get you and your Nearly-Wife to the ceremony, allow an extra fifteen

minutes on each trip in case there's traffic or some other hold-up on the road. Being early is okay: if you arrive early you'll have time up your sleeve to breathe and if she arrives early she can either do the same or do another couple of laps around the block. I arrived early and because the driveway was hidden from the chapel I had time to get out of the car and go to the bathroom for a last-minute toilet stop. Which, for me, was absolutely necessary (see On The Day, page 180)!

- Make sure there are no sporting or other public events scheduled on your wedding day that could disrupt your driver's route.

- Allow a standard ten minutes for your Nearly-Wife and her bridesmaids to get into the car on their way to the ceremony and ten minutes for them to get out of the car when they arrive. This will allow for the time it takes to arrange dresses, veils, bouquets, etc. Stop laughing – I'm serious.

- If you're being transported to a separate location for photos between the ceremony and the reception, closer to the day liaise between your photographer and driver to make sure they have each other's mobile numbers. If one or the other is unsure of the exact photo locations and they get lost, they can contact each other. Also, make sure you advise both your photographer and driver of exactly how long you want to spend taking photos and what time you need to be at your reception. If your photographer goes overtime and it results in your driver going beyond your agreed hire time, it will cost you as well as make you late.

- On that note, find out what the procedures are if you need to extend hire on the day. Will they have another wedding they need to rush off to? I'd strongly advise against booking a company that has another wedding on the same day as yours.
- If you're being picked up from your reception venue and transported to your wedding night accommodation: make sure your venue coordinator has your driver's number so they can contact them and advise them if the wedding's running over time and your pick-up time changes.
- Find out how your transport provider deals with extreme weather – do they provide umbrellas if it's raining or, if it's hot, do they have air-conditioning? Remember that most classic or vintage cars were built before aircon.
- Keep in contact with your transport provider to confirm your booking details and if any details change, notify them immediately in case they've made other bookings around yours.
- Closer to the day, ask your driver to make sure someone's got the rings the minute you get into the car!

THE CAKE

Not everyone who gets married has a wedding cake. Some people think they're tacky – one of my best friends didn't have a cake at her wedding because she didn't want any cheesy photos of her and her new husband posing with a knife.

The cake can also be one of the first things to go when couples are really looking to cut costs because they can be insanely expensive, especially the main-cake-with-individually-decorated-cupcakes style that has become very popular. The Bloke and I initially thought we wouldn't have a cake because we figured that desserts were already included in our reception package so what was the point of paying for another one? I know – we sound like massive hard-arses – but that was until we saw *it*.

I was googling away on my laptop while The Bloke and I sat in front of the telly one night (nothing like a couple who actually talk to each other of an evening, is there?) and, just for fun, I started looking at pictures of wedding cakes. Some were gorgeous, some were awful but one was so funny that I showed The Bloke and we immediately changed our minds about not having a cake.

It was a three-level yet still relatively small cake made to look like a bed with two levels leading up to it. Each level was strewn with discarded wedding clothes – tie, veil, suit, dress – and an empty champagne bottle, leading to the bed level where a nude couple sat on the edge of the bed wrapped only in a sheet. We loved it because it made us laugh and when we discovered that the cake-maker could also make a tiny Eddie Beagle to place on the lower level of the cake, we were goners. One white chocolate mud with a hint of citrus rudie-nudie wedding cake – sold to the couple on the couch who buy stuff on a whim.

I wouldn't advise ordering the first cake you see if you're trying to stick to a budget. Shopping around is smart because while styles can be similar from one cake-maker to the next, prices can vary wildly. And the best bit about shopping around for your wedding cake? You get to taste them all. Be as creative as you like when it comes to your cake flavour – gone are the days when everyone had fruitcake with thick sugared fondant icing, as evidenced by the last wedding I attended where they had the carrot cake with cream-cheese icing. Delicious.

Proof that alcohol, nudity and beagles do mix.

Whatever you do, don't trust any cake-maker who won't let you try before you buy. What you can trust them to do, however, is deliver the cake to your reception venue. This will usually incur a fee but if your cake has various layers or requires assembly of any kind, it's best to leave that to the experts. If you have a simple one-layer cake you can probably get away with arranging for a friend or family member to pick it up and deliver it for you. Actually, I'd advise two friends or family members: one to drive the car and one to make sure the cake doesn't slide around the back seat.

If you want to cut costs but still want a wedding cake, consider having your cake made by a local cake shop rather than a frou-frou wedding cake-maker because they'll charge you much less. Deciding whether your cake will be served as dessert, with coffee or as a take-home option will also determine your cake costs: dessert slices are cut larger than coffee slices, which are in turn roughly the same size as take-home slices. The larger the slice the bigger the cake you'll need to cover all your guests, which means the higher the cost. Note that take-home slices can also incur additional cost because you need to provide something for your guests to take their cake home in (usually either a box or a bag) although some wedding cake companies provide this and so do some reception venues.

And if you're planning on your cake being cut into take-home slices for your guests, make sure your guests actually get their cake. I've been to many weddings where there was so much cake left behind simply because guests weren't aware of where it was (quite common after 372 drinks). The best way to avoid this is to arrange with your reception venue for the cake to be left on guests' tables for them to take home. If the slices are being packaged and then placed somewhere for guests to collect, make sure your MC either announces this at some stage during the proceedings or the venue staff notify the guests at each table. Or you could hope that a conscientious friend steps in: one of my best friends was so alarmed by the fact that other guests had started leaving without taking their slice of wedding cake that she lifted the entire tray the bags were arranged on and served the remaining guests individually. Nice work.

BLOKE'S WORLD

The cake

You should definitely go with your Nearly-Wife when it comes to shopping around for your wedding cake and you should definitely do it on an empty stomach because you get to eat cake for free, making this one of the most fun parts of the planning process. And if you have an all-time favourite cake flavour this is your chance to lock it in for your wedding. If your cake has different layers or you're having cupcakes and you want one flavour but your Nearly-

Wife wants another, most cake-makers will let you mix and match so everybody's happy. And if you want them to, the really good ones will custom-design little figurines to look like you and your Nearly-Wife. Note: they won't always respond favourably to your requests for an enlargement of your figurine's 'package'.

Flavours you might think are awesome but which probably aren't suitable for your wedding cake include:

- Bourbon
- Dim sims
- Hommus
- Steak
- Potatoes
- Baked beans
- Gravy
- Bacon
- Corn chips
- Hotdog
- Popcorn chicken
- Your Nearly-Wife.

THE FOOD

There's a fair bit of cost-cutting talk in this book but one thing I believe you should never cut costs on at a wedding is the food. I don't know if my belief is grounded in my Greek heritage, where food is love ('Eat! You must eat!') or if it's the result of a wedding I once attended where they skimped on the food to the point where another guest was left feeling so hungry they had a pizza delivered to the reception. True (horror) story.

Regardless of what sort of wedding you're planning, it's a good idea to serve your guests some sort of food if you're planning on serving them alcohol (and if you're not planning on serving alcohol at your wedding, don't bother inviting me). Not serving food alongside the service of alcohol means you run the risk of guests drinking on an empty stomach, which has potential ramifications for people's blood alcohol levels when they drive home as well as for the pot plants in your venue (very popular spew destinations – don't ask me how I know).

When it came to our wedding food, The Bloke and I had a list of meals to choose from out of the three-course menu our venue provided for our sit-down dinner, which had the potential to be ridiculous. Let me explain: usually, when you're a guest at a wedding, the dinner staff will ask you 'Chicken or beef?' If The Bloke had his way, the staff at our wedding would have been asking 'Bacon or bacon?' The Bloke is in love with bacon. Seriously, if bacon was a woman who put out, the Bloke would not have married me.

I never fully understood the importance of bacon when I was single but since I've been with The Bloke I've learned that apparently it's integral to every single fricking meal. The Bloke would seriously eat bacon for breakfast, lunch and dinner if he could. Thank God he doesn't know how to make cocktails, because if he did we'd be drinking bacon daiquiris. And if we were wearing tracksuit pants while doing so, they'd be referred to as bacon tracky daiquiris. (You don't know how much I wanted to take the rest of the day off when I realised that.)

To give you an idea of how bacon has infiltrated my life thanks to The Bloke, there are certain things that I cook that never used to involve bacon that now feature bacon quite strongly. All my favourite vegetarian dishes now contain bacon. The chicken pie I used to make with puff pastry and a hint of rosemary? That's now a bacon pie with a hint of chicken. There's so much bacon on the table I might as well be living with Elvis.

It's not as if I haven't tried to restore the equilibrium. I love collecting cookbooks. Or as I like to call them, food porn. I can happily spend hours flicking through the glossy pages and salivating over the photography. I once tried to involve The Bloke in this pursuit in the hope that he might be inspired to think outside the bacon-flavoured square. He sat on the couch for half an hour looking more inspired with the turn of every page. Convinced he was being seduced by a world of non-bacon delicacies I asked what had taken his fancy for dinner. His answer: pancetta and pea risotto. Hooray for Italian bacon.

(I should take this moment to stress that I'm not in a 1950s-type relationship where I'm responsible for all the cooking. The Bloke loves to cook, but always with bacon. I actually limit his cooking privileges to weekends in order to guarantee I get five bacon-free nights every week.)

Of course, the downside to even two nights of bacon per week over a long period of time is weight gain. In the last few years I put on a bit of weight and while I've never really been overly body conscious, the extra padding shits me because now I can't fit in to some of my clothes (a pair of jeans that never used to give me a camel toe now give me a camel toe, which I think means I've even put on weight in my flange). But I started going to the gym a little while ago and The Bloke's been very supportive. The other night when we were walking the dog I sped up so I was walking a little further ahead. Then I asked The Bloke to have a look and tell me if my bum was getting any smaller, to which he replied, 'Yes . . . as you move further away.'

So, because of his obsession, The Bloke wanted bacon on the wedding menu but I didn't, because I just didn't think it was wedding food. I'd already chosen some dishes from the menu and because none of them involved bacon, The Bloke thought we should just add bacon to one. And the dish he thought we should add bacon to was penne pasta with rocket leaves, chilli, lemon and tuna.

My argument was that meat and fish weren't really meant for each other. His argument: 'What about "surf and turf" or "beef and reef"?'

So I told The Bloke I'd see his point and raise him a challenge: I'd let him add bacon to the tuna penne if he could come up with a way of rhyming pork with fish the same way beef's rhymed with reef and surf's rhymed with turf. And I was feeling pretty confident about that being an impossible thing to do until the bugger woke me up at 4 o'clock the next morning with the exclamation 'I've got it! Snout and trout!'

What are my options for wedding food?

The possibilities for wedding food depend on the type of wedding you're having and the location. For example, the food you'd serve for a sit-down dinner would be different to the food served at a cocktail reception. If you're having your reception at a favourite restaurant, high-five yourself because the last thing you'll have to worry about is whether or not your food's going to be any good. Unless you're having your reception at one of the restaurants from Gordon Ramsay's *Kitchen Nightmares*, in which case, my condolences.

If you're having your reception at a reception centre or any other function centre, you'll find that most of these places include food as part of their package. This is great because it saves you from having to book a separate caterer. However, it also means you're at the mercy of their in-house chef and here's where you need to be careful. If the food that you're going to serve at your wedding is important to you, INSIST that you be allowed to taste-test. Don't just rely on the pictures they show you in their brochures. Despite the fact that there's no guarantee you're going to be served food that looks identical anyway, what if it looks okay but tastes like slop?

Ask whether they have food-sampling evenings for prospective clients. These are also good once you've actually booked your venue and you're trying to decide on exactly which of their dishes you'd like to serve to your guests. Remember that everything will sound delicious thanks to a few well-chosen adjectives on their menu – it's what it actually looks and tastes like that's important. And make sure you ask about children's meals, vegetarian options and whether they cater for food allergies.

If your reception is being held somewhere that requires you to hire your own caterer and you don't know where to start, ask around. Better to start off with someone's recommendation than choose blind and you never know who might have hired the most fantastic caterer in the last year or so. Again, make a list of prospective caterers and meet with them to discuss your needs and budget.

Topics for discussion should include: how many events they cater for per day (too many and their resources will be stretched); how much input you can have into the menu; whether they cater for special food requirements such as vegetarians or coeliacs; whether they also look after the bar requirements; how many staff members will be there to serve; and what infrastructure they supply (plates, glasses, cutlery, tables, chairs, etc.). Asking for references is pretty standard in the catering industry so again, make sure you get a list of recent weddings and contact details. And don't forget to sign a contract once you've chosen your caterer to lock in their availability for your big day.

BLOKE'S WORLD

Wedding Food

I know it's just as much your wedding as it is your Nearly-Wife's, but there are some things you should probably let go of when it comes to the food served at your wedding reception. Someone wise once told me that one of the secrets to a great marriage is to pick your battles and I'd argue that the same goes here. Do what you like at your next barbecue but in the interests of harmony and your chances of pre-marital sex I'd advise paying attention to the following tips when it comes to your wedding:

Five things you should remember when helping your fiancée plan the food for your reception:

1. Melted cheese is not one of the five food groups.
2. 'Twiggy sticks' are not canapés. Twiggy sticks are Shmackos for humans.
3. You may love Cheese 'n' Bacon Balls but that doesn't mean they're appropriate finger food.
4. You're allowed one inappropriate joke about the phrase 'finger food'.
5. Dessert should never involve Milo.

WEDDING FAVOURS

If you're like me and you thought the term 'wedding favours' referred to what happened between the bride and groom on their wedding night, look sharp.

Wedding favours are the little gift of thanks your guests get to take home from your wedding so that they'll have something to remember your wedding by. Usually it's something tangible like a little candle or a jar of lollies as opposed to something intangible like an enjoyable evening or salmonella poisoning. Wedding favours used to be called bonbonnière and were based on the European tradition of giving guests a little box of sugared almonds, which symbolised the bittersweet nature of marriage (don't ask). The box usually contained three or five sugared almonds: three represented the bride, groom and their future child, and five represented health, wealth, happiness, fertility and long life. I'm buggered if I know when or why 'bonbonnière' changed to 'wedding favours' but I'm tipping it probably had something to do with commercialisation or maybe some kind of anti-wog backlash.

Wedding favours provide you with another chance to put a personal stamp on your wedding, but be mindful of the fact that they also provide the potential for budget blow-out depending on the wedding favour you choose. A small jar of lollies is reasonable, a small basket of hand-made Belgian chocolates straight from Belgium with your photo on the wrapper is probably going a bit overboard. Then again, it all depends on your budget and the number of guests you have to allow for: if you're having a small wedding and your budget allows for it you can probably afford to spend more on your wedding favours if you want to. Searching for wedding favours on the net will give you a good idea of what's out there and the pricing involved. Just bear in mind that wedding favours are intended to be a symbolic gesture of appreciation to your guests rather than a grand expression of thanks.

Do I have To have wedding favours?

Fair question. In the words of The Bloke, who was always a bit mystified as to why we were giving our guests wedding favours: 'Aren't we already feeding them and getting them drunk?' Wedding favours are traditional but ultimately it's your wedding and no, you don't have to have them if you don't want to. However, if you're a creative person wedding favours can be a great outlet for creative expression because you can tailor your wedding favours to your wedding location, to how you and your Almost-Husband met, or to your professions, hobbies or personalities. For example:

- Wine bottle-stoppers – great if your wedding's being held at a winery, not that great if a significant proportion of your guests belong to AA.
- Stubby holders – could reflect the fact that you and your Almost-Husband love having BBQs or the fact that you both just really like beer. Great for casual, laid-back weddings, not so great for formal occasions.
- Shot glasses – a nod to the fact that you and your Almost-Husband met at a bar or to the fact that your signature cocktail at the reception will actually be tequila shots.
- Key chains – did I hear someone say swingers' party?
- Luggage tag – you love to travel and remember the days when flying Qantas didn't involve praying first.
- Tea-light candle holder – you know your guests look better without harsh lighting.

- Soaps – you or your guests stink. I'm serious. No, I'm not.
- Beach-themed favours such as shell-shaped magnets or candles – cute for seaside weddings.
- Mini photo-frames – you and your Almost-Husband are photographers. Or framers.
- Bookmarks – you're librarians. Or maybe you once did it in a library?

I liked the idea of wedding favours so I talked The Bloke into giving our guests a small jar of lollies from a company called Suga. Each lolly had our names on it and the lolly colours matched the tones used in our invitation. We further personalised the lolly jars by covering the lids with a little square of ivory satin (so they toned in with everything else that would be sitting on our guests' tables) and using ribbon to attach a little tag bearing the sunset photo from our invitation and our wedding date. When this was at the ideas stage, The Bloke thought it was all a bit naff. Amazing how that changed when he realised he could not only choose our lolly flavours but that this would also involve a lengthy visit to Suga for taste-testing.

Altogether, our wedding favours cost us approximately $400, which equated to roughly $3 per guest. In hindsight, they would have cost us less if we'd sourced our own containers and less again if we hadn't done the satin-ribbon-tag thing. In any case, however, they looked and tasted great!

HOW CAN I SAVE MONEY ON MY WEDDING FAVOURS?

If you want to have wedding favours but also want to cut your costs, making them yourself can save you heaps of cash – the only downside being that this will take up more of your time. The good news here is that DIY wedding favours give you the opportunity to invite bridesmaids, friends or family round to your place for an afternoon of helping you make them (and drinking champagne). It's also a really good job for stay-at-home mothers-of-the-bride with creative flair: show them what you need done and leave them to it – if they've offered to help, they'll love this. I even know of a father-of-the-groom who made all his son's wedding favours because he was recently retired and needed something to keep him busy. What a cool dad.

If you're going to make your own wedding favours, ensure you make them well enough in advance so you're not stressing about them two days before your wedding. Aim to have them ready at least two weeks before your wedding date – this means you can drop them off to your venue a week before your wedding or still have a week up your sleeve if you're running behind.

Ideas for do-it-yourself wedding favours:

- Lollies, mints, nuts, cookies or chocolates. You can put them in tins, Asian-inspired take-away boxes, jars, boxes, little silver pails, mugs or organza bags (or any other fabric bags, for that matter). Craft shops are a great place to source materials but you'll also be surprised at what you can find in discount 'two-dollar' shops, especially in the organza bag department. If you're having a big wedding you can also get significant discounts for bulk orders through online stores.

- A small card designed and printed so that it ties in with the colour theme of your wedding, with a foil-wrapped chocolate or cookie attached to it.
- Mini bottles of port, liqueur or wine.
- Potpourri bags or sachets, but only if you're going to use decent potpourri – you don't want your reception venue smelling like a toilet once they've all been laid out on the tables.
- Seed packets, seedlings or even spring bulbs are increasingly popular and eco-friendly wedding favour ideas that are easy to put together yourself but, in the case of seedlings, you need to make sure you've done them far enough in advance for them to have sprouted for your wedding.
- A personalised CD including special songs, funny songs (see the next chapter) and songs from your wedding (e.g. processional song, first dance song, etc.). These are extra special when you and your Almost-Husband take the time to record a little intro.

- You can also customise anything you haven't actually made yourself. For example, you could print your names and your wedding date on a stubby holder or you could personalise practically anything else by tying on a little tag with your names and wedding date, or printing little labels or stickers.

Making your wedding favours double as place cards is another way to cut costs. For example, if you're having mini photo frames as your wedding favours, have them contain a piece of paper with your guests' names printed on it. Just make sure there's a little note on each table letting your guests know they can take them home – I once went to a wedding where many people just assumed the frames belonged to the reception venue and left them on the tables. (Another way to get around this would be to have something like 'A gift to thank you for sharing our special day' also written on the paper in the frames to make it clear to your guests that you want them to take them home.) You can also make other wedding favours double as place cards by attaching a little tag or label with guests' names to each favour – just make sure these are easy to see when your guests get to their tables.

BLOKE'S WORLD

Wedding favours

If you think wedding favours are a bit girly, consider this: you could have his & hers wedding favours. You choose the little gift for your male guests, your Nearly-Wife chooses the little gift for your female guests. So you might end up with something like stubby-holders for the guys and fragrance sachets for the girls. It's a little bit 'battle of the sexes' but it's an option, right?

If you're going to choose the guys' gifts, just bear in mind that the following items are probably not considered appropriate as wedding favours, no matter how much you personalise them:

- Condoms
- Lube
- Copies of that episode of *The Footy Show* where Sam Newman got his cock out
- *Ralph* magazine
- Photos from your bucks' night (I don't care how big her boobs were)
- Live bait
- Your list of 'World Of Warcraft' tactics
- Bongs (yes, even bucket-bongs)
- Viagra.

Other than that, feel free to use your imagination.

THE MUSIc

Music is a really important part of a wedding because the songs a couple choose for their ceremony and reception can tell you a lot about them and their relationship. I once went to a wedding where the groom surprised the bride by singing her a song at the reception. Which was a lovely gesture, but he sang something that sent the bride a very clear message about how he wanted their marriage to be. He sang her a song called 'You Say It Best When You Say Nothing At All'. And that probably would have been okay if she was a mute, but she wasn't. In fact, I got the distinct impression that if that groom had been able to sing her a song called 'Just Shut The Fuck Up', he would have.

You might already have a special song that you want to play for your first dance together at the reception but there are other parts of your wedding that can be greatly enhanced by music that you've specifically chosen. Most people forgo the traditional Wedding March nowadays and walk down the aisle to something more personal – which brings us to the most important factor in choosing music: it should be about songs that are significant to you, not songs that you think your guests would like to hear. They don't even have to be songs that your guests have ever heard before, or in the case of the song I walked down the aisle to, songs that are in English. My processional (walking down the aisle) song was called 'Hoppipolla' and it's by Icelandic band Sigur Ros. Long before we married, The Bloke found it and said he'd love to see me walk down the aisle to it. He then followed that beautiful sentiment up by saying, 'Provided that your husband lets me come to your wedding'. Smart arse.

We found a translation of the lyrics and learned that it's about reliving childhood by jumping in puddles, getting nosebleeds and spinning round and round in circles. The film clip features a bunch of old people playing children's games. It's got about as much to do with getting married as 'Tie Me Kangaroo Down, Sport' but I loved it and loved that The Bloke thought about marrying me when he heard it, so that was that.

Other places to put music in your ceremony include the interlude when you're signing your wedding certificate. This can take longer than you might think so you might even want to put two songs here – if you're finished before the end of the second song you can just have whoever's operating your music fade it out. And a recessional song – the song that plays you out of the church or ceremony venue – is a great place to play something really happy.

The Bloke and I used 'Two Wooden Spoons' by This Is The Kit and 'Wonderful' by Josh Rouse for when we were signing our certificate, and 'All I Want Is You' by Barry Louis Polisar as our recessional song – it's the song that plays right at the beginning of the movie *Juno*. Movie soundtracks are a great resource when you're looking for songs. The other two songs I found by listening to a bunch of CDs I'd been given when I worked at Triple J and had never found the time to listen to. If you don't have songs already picked out, listening over CDs you haven't heard for a while or borrowing CDs from friends can be really helpful, because often it's not until you're listening to find something that suits an express purpose that you discover something you like.

Aside from what your band or DJ plays for your guests to dance to, there are ample opportunities to enhance your reception with specifically chosen tracks, too. A song to play your bridal party into the reception venue as they're being presented can really set the mood – choose something upbeat and vibrant to build towards you being presented next. Our bridal party was presented to the cranked-up sounds of Curtis

Mayfield's 'Move On Up'. After they made their entrance there was a pause (to build anticipation – it's all about the vibe, baby!) then The Bloke and I walked in to The Beatles 'All You Need Is Love'. Shmaltzy? Maybe a little. But I defy you to listen to those opening strains of brass and drums and not get a little shiver. We also used this song to play us out of the reception when we made our exit at the end of the night, which was really cool because by that stage all our guests were pissed and they actually sang it to us. This was one of my favourite moments – consider the lyrics then imagine 130 of your nearest and dearest singing it to you after you've just got married and you'll understand why.

You can also have fun with the music you use at your wedding. I'll never forget the wedding I attended where the bride and groom walked into their reception to 'The Imperial March' (Darth Vader's theme) from *Star Wars*, because I nearly fell off my chair laughing. Likewise the wedding where the bridal couple walked in to the theme from *Rocky* while punching the air and high-fiving their guests as they made their way past. Priceless.

The song that you play for your first dance together depends on what sort of dance you'll be doing. The bridal waltz isn't always a waltz anymore. I've seen Latin dancing, swing dancing, the tango, ballroom dancing, and a great clip on YouTube where the bride and groom learned every single dance step to Sir Mix-A-Lot's 'Baby Got Back (I Like Big Butts)'. Seriously. Google it. Dancing lessons are worth the money if you don't know how to dance – The Bloke and I had lessons in a style known as Ceroc (it has elements of Latin, ballroom and dirty dancing – but not too dirty) and not only did they make us feel much more confident when it came to our big moment but the lessons were fun and a great 'time-out' from the busy-ness we felt in the couple of weeks leading up to the wedding. We both have two left feet, so if you're worried about your ability to dance rest assured that it only took us six lessons – if we can do it, anyone can. We danced to a song called 'Fee Fie' by The Hidden Cameras. See what I mean about your songs not having to mean a thing to anyone else but you?

There are plenty of great songs to choose from for your ceremony and reception. Here's a list of some that you should probably avoid:

'Dude Looks Like A Lady' – Aerosmith
'Murder On The Dance Floor' – Sophie Ellis Bextor
'Am I Ever Gonna See Your Face Again' – The Angels
'Don't Stand So Close To Me' – The Police
'I Touch Myself' – The Divinyls
'Suspicious Minds' – Elvis Presley
'The Bitch Is Back' – Elton John
'Dickhead' – Kate Nash

'The Lady Is A Tramp' – Frank Sinatra
The theme from *The Crying Game*
'I Like It Both Ways' – Supernaut
'Killing In The Name Of' –
    Rage Against The Machine
'Where's Your Head At' – Basement Jaxx
'Asshole' – Denis Leary
'Every Day I Love You Less And Less' –
    The Kaiser Chiefs
'Smack My Bitch Up' – The Prodigy
'She Bangs' – Ricki Martin
'Womanizer' – Britney Spears
'Closer' (I Wanna Fuck You Like An Animal) –
    Nine Inch Nails

THE RECEPTION

 In terms of what it felt like to me, my wedding day went like this:

Getting ready at my parents' place . . . took forever

Driving to the ceremony . . . took forever

The ceremony . . . didn't take too long but felt slow, like a dream

Official photos . . . didn't take too long, lots of fun

The reception . . . what reception? My God, did I just have a reception?

Even though it will go for a few hours your reception will feel like it's over in a flash. (Hopefully your wedding night won't follow suit.) But don't worry – this seems to be the case for everybody. My favourite description of what having a wedding reception feels like came courtesy of a friend who said that most of his recollections were 'just a blur of colours and happiness'.

Your wedding reception is your chance to really celebrate your marriage with your new husband, your family and your friends. Regardless of what kind of reception you're having (lunch, cocktail, sit-down dinner, etc.), there are a number of reception features you might choose to include, such as an official entrance of the bridal party, an official entrance of the newlyweds, speeches and toasts, dancing (bridal waltz, dancing with parents, traditional dancing, etc.), cutting the cake, throwing the bouquet or garter and an official farewell to and exit of the newlyweds as well as any traditional customs that are part of your heritage, such as a tea-ceremony, traditional dancing or plate-smashing.

(Before you ask, no I didn't have any plate-smashing at my wedding. I'm not quite that traditional. Plus, I'm a neat-freak Virgo. Can you imagine how apoplectic I'd get at the sight of 130 people all smashing perfectly good crockery? We did have Greek dancing, though, and one of my favourite memories of the reception is when I looked up from the dance floor and realised that all the dinner tables were empty because almost every single guest – wog, non-wog and even elderly – was on the dance floor with me, arm in arm and dancing Zorba.)

You can have as many or as few reception formalities as you like. For instance, rather than have a bouquet-toss, I presented my flowers to my parents, and seeing as my garter belonged to The Bloke's grandmother and was technically a family heirloom, we thought it best that it remained safely hidden under my dress and away from speccy-taking guests.

Drawing up a running order for your reception will help ensure you fit everything in and still allow yourself enough time to relax with your new husband and guests. Personally, I'm no stranger to running orders because I've had to adhere to them over the years when I've done gigs and been part of shows. And in an odd way, drawing up the running order for a wedding reception is a bit like drawing up the running order for a show: you include all the entrances, the exits and all the features and formalities in between with enough time for drinks, toilet breaks and the occasional heckle.

The best way to draw up your running order is for you and your Almost-Husband to decide on all the formalities you'd like to have happen (such as speeches, dances, etc.) and then confer with your venue coordinator to schedule these features around the ones that have to happen (such as service of various food and drink courses, etc.). This will ensure that there's a reasonable amount of space between all your courses to accommodate serving, eating and clearing allowances. It will also help achieve a good balance between the time allocated for formalities and the time allocated for partying or relaxing.

Here are some tips for your running order:

- Give a copy of your running order to your MC a few days before the wedding and go over it with them so they know what's happening and when. It's also a good idea to ensure your DJ or band has a copy so they know when to strike up music for dancing and/or entrances, introductions for speakers and exits.
- Consider scheduling the speeches early. Your speakers will be grateful to get them out of the way and minimise the time they spend feeling nervous about speaking in front of a crowd (and holding off on their enjoyment of the free drinks before they do). Having speeches earlier rather than later also means speakers won't have consumed as much alcohol as they might have towards the end of night, limiting your chances of ending up with drunk or rambling epics.
- Similarly, if you're nervous about doing your bridal waltz then get that out of the way early, too. No point stressing about it for the whole night. I once went to a wedding where the couple made their official entrance to the opening strains of their bridal waltz song. They headed straight to the dance floor and immediately began their first dance as husband and wife. It looked like a scene from a film and you would never have guessed it was all because

they just wanted to get their dance over and done with.

- If your reception venue isn't centrally located, consider putting a 'taxi announcement' into your running order. My wedding venue coordinator advised us that it took taxis at least forty-five minutes to arrive at our venue after they were booked. We scheduled a taxi-announcement for our guests an hour before the end of our reception so their night wouldn't end with them waiting ages for a cab. The taxi announcement simply involved the MC saying something along the lines of 'Due to the delays often experienced in getting taxis to the top of Mount Dandenong, may I suggest that guests wishing to travel home by cab please make their calls to their preferred taxi company now.' Not particularly glamorous but very much appreciated by guests who didn't have their night spoiled by having to spend an hour out in the cold.

Who Should I have as my MC?

A good MC is incredibly important to a great reception because they have to make sure that everything happens when it's supposed to as well as make your guests feel warmly welcomed and entertained. Because the MC has to be on top of both tasks at the same time, it's a position that involves a fair amount of pressure, skill and responsibility. Some reception venues provide their own MC (often the venue's coordinator) or you can choose a trusted friend or family member. For example, my dad has been the MC at quite a few weddings for various relatives over the years because it's something he enjoys and more importantly, he's natural about it and makes sure he does a good job (there must be public speaking and performance skills in the Psiakis genes). Although every time Dad opens with a joke (and he does), I pray to God it's not the one about the constipated accountant (see Setting the Date, page 32).

Because the tasks involved in the role of MC are actually quite distinct – one's a bit showbiz while the other is almost purely administrative – The Bloke and I followed the brilliant suggestion of our venue coordinator and chose to have joint MCs. Our 'administrative MC' was our venue coordinator and he took care of the business and housekeeping side of the reception by announcing entrances and exits, the cutting of the cake, dancing, and the taxi call. He also formally introduced our 'showbiz MC,' a great friend and stand-up comedian who made a welcoming speech and MC'd the speeches and toasts by introducing all our official speakers.

Having joint MCs worked really well for us and I think it's a terrific idea because it means that the administrative side of all your formalities can be taken care of by an administrator who's done it all a thousand times before while the showbiz side can be taken care of by someone whose only job is to be welcoming, personable and entertaining. Even if this person isn't a professional performer, their job is automatically made so much easier because their involvement only covers one part of the night (which means they get to relax for the rest of it) and they only have to concentrate on the fun side of things rather than worrying about all the boring stuff. Nobody gets excited about having to tell people when to call a cab.

Regardless of how many MCs you decide to have, before asking them to do the job you should be confident that the person (or people) you choose can demonstrate the following:

- A sound understanding of what it is they're expected to do
- Good public speaking skills
- The ability to be warm and friendly and make all your guests feel welcome
- The ability to keep proceedings moving and running to time
- Sensitivity towards what is and isn't appropriate to say at a wedding
- The ability to stay sober from the beginning until the end of their responsibilities.

In the interests of balance, it's probably best not to choose anyone who displays any of these attributes:

- Tendency to projectile vomit in the middle of sentences
- Pathological fear of microphones, microphone stands or lecterns
- Tendency towards inappropriate erections or spontaneous indecent exposure
- Tendency towards a distinct overuse of the phrase 'Well, fuck me dead and call me Elroy'.

There's a traditional order and content for wedding speeches that your venue coordinator will be able to help you with and if you or any of your speakers are unsure about anything to do with this there's also a wealth of information and examples on the internet. Looking at other people's wedding speeches is actually a really good way to get a sense of exactly what should be included as well as the tone that's required. Just make sure you discourage your speakers from taking the cheat's way out and copying someone else's speech word for word (or at least make sure they change the names if they do). And above all, ensure they understand that the time limit you set for their speech is final and there'll be hell to pay and no wedding cake for them if they don't stick to it.

Do I hAvE To MAKE A sPEech As well?

Traditionally, only the groom makes a speech at the wedding reception but have a guess what I think about that. It still happens occasionally but I've also been to weddings where the bride and the groom each made separate speeches as well as weddings where they spoke together. The Bloke and I chose the latter option because we liked the idea of one of our first official duties as a married couple being to make a joint speech expressing our thanks to our family and friends.

Whatever option you choose, my advice would be for you and/or your Almost-Husband to start thinking about your speech a couple of weeks before the big day. It's an important part of the proceedings and while it doesn't necessarily have to be totally scripted, it's not the sort of thing you want to leave to the last minute and have regrets about later. And don't worry if neither of you are expert speech-makers: nobody expects you to be. All people expect is for you to speak from the heart, which isn't really that hard because it's an emotional occasion anyway. Although your speech doesn't have to be mawkish or sentimental – it can be funny and sweet or whatever else you want it to be.

Initially, The Bloke wasn't looking forward to writing our speech because he said he had no idea what to say. We found that sitting down together (wine!) and talking about everything we were grateful for and the people we wanted to take the opportunity to recognise helped us form a list of points that then became the foundation of our speech. We wrote it together, delegated which one of us would say which bits and then wrote the last little part where we thanked each other separately so that those words would be a surprise to each other on the night.

WHAT CAN I DO TO MAKE SURE I ENJOY MY RECEPTION AS MUCH AS POSSIBLE?

Wear flat shoes. I'm serious. Many a bride has quietly slipped on a pair of dainty thongs or ballet slippers at her reception without anyone else noticing and enjoyed an evening of complete and utter comfort. The really kind ones even buy pairs for their bridesmaids. If the dresses are long, *no-one will ever know*.

When you and your new husband have worked super-hard trying to organise and personalise every single detail of your wedding, sometimes the hardest thing to do is actually relax and enjoy it but it's something I highly recommend. Hell, you've paid for enough of it so you might as well get your money's worth! Here are some tips to help both you and your Almost-Husband enjoy the fruit of your wedding-planning labours:

- If you're massive stress-heads and paranoid that somewhere along the line, someone's going to fuck up and forget something, take one big opportunity to put your mind at rest. When you first arrive at your reception you usually get a little private time for refreshments and the like in the bridal lounge before you're officially presented to the rest of your guests. If you're totally wigged out, use this time to ask a minion to quickly assemble your venue coordinator, your MC, your head caterer (if you have one) your DJ or band-leader, your speech-makers and anyone else who has a special role at the reception and do one quick final check of whatever's nagging at your brain. Do this briefly and ONCE ONLY at the start of the reception and it will save you from spending the rest of it flitting back and forth to all these people to check that they know what you want them to do, you crazy control-freaks. What? Nothing.

- Make sure you both get to eat. You might not have time to get through all of each course what with all the mingling you have to do but at least try and get a few mouthfuls. Not only will this save you from falling over due to low blood sugar combined with alcohol but when the wedding's over and you're at your hotel or wherever it's fun to say things like 'Gee, I'm glad we put rack of lamb on the menu – that lick of it that I had was delicious!'

- By all means try and get around to mingling with all your guests but if it gets to half an hour before the reception ends and you have the choice between mingling with the last few people you haven't spoken to yet or having a dance with each other and the guests on the dance floor, have a dance. People will forgive you for wanting to enjoy your own wedding and it's not every day you get to do the 'Nutbush' with your grandmothers.

- Take a few mental pictures. As talented as they might be, your photographer won't be able to capture the sound of the animated chatter and laughter of all your guests ringing out throughout the room, the smell of the flowers in your bouquet and buttonhole, the feel of all your wedding finery against your skin or the tingle in your tummy when you grin at each other while everything else around you unfolds. You have to register those things for yourselves as they happen because once the reception's over, the only place you'll be able to recreate those things the exact way they happened will be in your memories.

- Similarly, take some time out with each other away from everyone else. Not so much that people start wondering where the hell you are but a few minutes here and there where you can either stand somewhere quiet to take in the scenes around you or slip away outside for a few moments together.

The Bloke and I tried to do this a few times throughout the night and my favourite little retreat was when we met up in our bridal lounge and did our bridal waltz alone, without the music. Yep. Probably one of the most romantic moments of my life. (And who knew that the 19-year-old venue employee would be right about us needing a private area where the two of us could go to 'get away from' all our guests?)

Now, let's all have a drink!

PART

3$^1/_2$

The aftermath . . .

THE WEDDING NIGHT

No, this chapter will not feature diagrams and graphics that I've lifted from the *Kama Sutra* or *The Joy Of Sex*. Especially not *The Joy Of Sex*. Apparently there's a new, updated edition but I don't need to see it – the shaggy couple shagging in the 1972 edition will stay with me for life.

My wedding night started very soon after The Bloke and I left our wedding, which sounds saucy but what I mean is that it only took us a few minutes to get from our reception to our wedding night accommodation, where our wedding night officially began. We were staying in a cottage down the road and when we left our reception, the clock on the car's dashboard said 10.02 pm. When we arrived it said 10.07 pm. Not bad!

The Bloke had chosen our accommodation and it was gorgeous: a modern one-bedroom, tri-level cottage set right into a fern gully in the Dandenongs. It had huge windows to capture the view, was surrounded by trees and we felt like we were in the treetops. With our wedding finishing so early (due to the fact that it was a Sunday night reception) and arriving at our accommodation so quickly, we felt like we still had a whole night ahead of us so we opened a bottle of champagne, put on some music and sat on the couch in front of the wood stove. We talked for two hours about our favourite moments from the wedding and everything else that had happened that day and it was so nice to just relax together. The Bloke didn't even flick on the telly to watch sport.

Before we settled in on the couch The Bloke had showed no hesitation towards getting out of his suit and into his bog-catcher tracky-dacks (so romantic), but I was reluctant to take off my dress. I remember thinking that I didn't want to take it off because the moment I did, our wedding would officially be over and I'd never get another chance to wear something so beautiful ever again. It's not exactly the kind of outfit you can pop on for a quick trip down the shops.

When it came time to go to bed, I finally took off my dress. I carefully placed it on a hanger, which I then hung from the curtain rail running along the huge window next to our bed. Because the dress was completely framed by the window, with its long skirt just skimming the floor and the moonlight shining in behind it from outside, the whole thing looked like a picture and the impact wasn't lost on The Bloke. When he walked into the room he stopped and just stared at the dress, making me think that perhaps he too had been struck by the effect. Instead he squinted, pointed and then said, 'This is going to sound a little weird but is that a tiny pair of scissors I can see?'

TIPS FOR YOUR WEDDING NIGHT

No, I'm not going to give you any sex tips here, these are just logistical tips (the sex tips are in a couple of pages!)

- Have everything you need in the way of clothing, toiletries etc., delivered to your wedding night accommodation before you get there rather than trying to take them there with you from your reception. Arrange for someone to drop your bags off at your accommodation on the day of the wedding – this means that everything you need will be waiting for you when you arrive and you'll have one less thing to worry about on the day. Even if you're staying at a hotel and your room isn't necessarily ready when your gear gets dropped off, the concierge can have your bags put in there the minute it is.

- As well as clothing and toiletries, don't forget to pack any other things you might want on your wedding night, including music, lingerie, candles, luxury bath products, aromatherapy oil, contraception, a live goat, etc. Of course I'm joking about the goat (or am I?) but in the rush of packing the other stuff is often forgotten until you arrive.

- Don't forget to pack garment bags for your suit and dress so they can be protected when you take them home rather than just bundled into a suitcase or flung over a car seat.

- If you're staying somewhere that doesn't do late room service or indeed any room service, organise for some food to be at your accommodation. You usually don't get time to eat much at the reception and if you're anything like me, you'll be starving once you get to where you're spending the night. Our best man and his girlfriend were kind enough to arrange for a hamper of food and drink to be waiting for us at our cottage and we tore into it when we arrived. If you don't have room service at your accommodation, it's also great to have breakfast supplies waiting for you so that everything's there when you need it in the morning.

- Arrange for a late checkout and don't forget to hang the 'Do Not Disturb' sign on the door.

THE SEX BIT

Ordinarily I wouldn't presume to give anyone advice about sex but some things are too funny to ignore. While trawling the internet in the lead-up to my wedding day, I came across a wedding website that offered wedding night sex tips and they made me laugh so much I thought I'd share them with you here:

Tip: Talk to your partner about what he has in mind for your wedding night, including any special place he wants to be. I think we all know what he's got in mind and where he's going to want to be.

Tip: Wear something your partner has never seen you in before to create some mystery and interest. What – like a Sherlock Holmes costume?

Tip: If you've been living together, stay away from each other for a week at least. Um, I'm tipping that'll be tricky if you're living together . . .

Tip: If you're virgins, take it slowly. If you're virgins, take it any way you can!

Tip: Try something new – your wedding night can be a fun time to experiment. Yeah, so don't forget to pack a Bunsen burner and a wad of litmus paper.

Tip: Accept the fact that you may be too exhausted or tipsy to have sex. Likewise, accept the fact that if you fall asleep while on the job you'll never hear the end of it for the rest of your marriage.

BLOKE'S WORLD

The wedding night

The Bloke consistently referred to our wedding night as the 'business-end of the wedding.' While this never failed to disturb me somewhat, I was grateful for The Bloke's being adamant that the 'business-end' should be his responsibility. He was of the opinion that since I had things to organise that he didn't, such as hair and make-up trials and bookings for the big day, he should take on organising the wedding night as a way of making sure we each had roughly the same number of things to do. I can't tell you how much I appreciated this gesture and honestly, I highly recommend that you consider doing the same. I can pretty much guarantee your Nearly-Wife will be grateful. *Very* grateful (if you're picking up what I'm putting down).

Consider keeping your wedding night destination a secret and making the whole thing a surprise – read the logistical tips above so you can organise for the delivery of your belongings and some food. Provided the surprise doesn't turn out to be the fact that you'll be spending your first night together in the club rooms of your favourite footy club, your Nearly-Wife will be grateful. *Very* grateful. (Are you picking up on a theme?)

Regardless of how far your wedding night accommodation is from your reception venue, make all your transport arrangements well in advance and consider booking a car with a driver rather than a taxi (it's your wedding, after all). Even if you do end up travelling by taxi, making and confirming your booking in advance will mean you won't be stuck waiting around at the reception. Not having to suffer the indignity of waving guests off as they leave in their pre-ordered cabs while you wait for yours will definitely make your Nearly-Wife feel grateful. *Very* grateful. (Look, if you want a good time on your wedding night, do everything you can to organise a corker!)

Finally, do not under any circumstances turn on the television on your wedding night. Even using the excuse, 'You looked so beautiful today I just want to see if our wedding made the late news,' won't work, especially when the time you flick on the telly just happens to coincide with the beginning of *Sports Tonight*. I'm on to you, buddy.

THE HONEYMOON

The Bloke and I are really into supporting local tourism so when it came to planning our honeymoon, we decided to stay in the country (translation: we don't have passports). Our criteria for a perfect honeymoon destination was as follows:

- It had to be in a warm and sunny location near the beach
- It had to have full kitchen facilities because we love cooking
- It had to be in the vicinity of restaurants and cafés for when we got sick of cooking
- It had to be somewhere where we didn't need a car on a day-to-day basis
- It had to have pay-TV for watching sport (The Bloke's requirement)

- It had to be private accommodation so we didn't have to 'DWD' (deal with dickheads – my requirement).

With two-and-bit weeks up our sleeve we decided to do a week in one place, a week in another and then spend a few days in Port Fairy, which we knew wouldn't be warm and sunny but given that The Bloke's family has a house there, we knew that it would be free (and still close to the beach). After realising that in May/June, the only warm and sunny location near a beach was probably Queensland, we chose Palm Cove and Port Douglas as our honeymoon destinations.

Far North Queensland (or FNQ if you want it to sound mildly offensive) is truly delightful. There are so many things to love about Queensland. There's the sun, the sand, the surf, and the company that sells ice from service stations called 'Cousins Ice'. In two weeks, The Bloke and I didn't see a single sign that hadn't been scrawled over so that it said 'Ben Cousins' Ice' and I don't care what you think, that's funny. One of them even had the apostrophe in the right place. (Correct grammar is, I feel, integral to the defacing of someone else's property.)

When it came to finding accommodation up north, we quickly decided to steer clear of the big resorts. Sure they're luxurious and decadent and you should spoil yourself on your honeymoon but after all the money we'd just spent on the wedding, they were a little too luxurious and decadent. I was also keen to stay in private accommodation where we didn't have to share any facilities. Call me antisocial (because I often am), but I couldn't think of anything worse than getting stuck in awkward social situations. You always hear those honeymoon stories where people go, 'Yeah, we stayed in a beautiful resort up north but we met this nightmare couple by the pool one day and they joined us for dinner that night and from that point on we just couldn't get rid of them. When they asked for our number to catch up if they were ever in Melbourne down the track, we gave them a fake one. We feel terrible.' The reality is that these people actually don't feel terrible because the reality is also that some people are just complete knobs who need to be beaten away with a big stick. I'm talking to you, loud and obnoxious touristy-types! (Yep, definitely antisocial.)

Ruling out resorts meant looking for a private little house or cottage to rent so we turned to an accommodation website we'd used many times in the past that has never let us down. It's called stayz.com.au (don't let the whacky 'z' put you off) and it's a national database for all kinds of different accommodation types and budgets. There's also a pet-friendly section if you want to take your dog or cat (we didn't take

Eddie because he has a fear of flying. Seriously, he's afraid of flying and the 'Stars Without Make-up' edition of *New Weekly*).

We decided that our week in Palm Cove would be our luxury week (within reason) so we rented a house about a block from the main street, which runs along the beach. The house had a huge inground pool surrounded by lush gardens so it was like being in our own private resort. It had pay-TV and we were within walking distance of everything we needed. It was perfect, and even now whenever I'm feeling stressed I close my eyes and imagine being back there . . . and in charge of the remote.

For our week in Port Douglas we rented a small townhouse. It had a little pool and everything else we needed in the house but it was a bit further from the main street and the beach. Luckily, bikes and helmets were included with the property and The Bloke and I had a great time riding everywhere, especially along Four Mile Beach. And it certainly made us realise how long it had been since we'd both ridden bikes – talk about saddle-sore! Here's a tip: when your mum calls to ask how you're enjoying your honeymoon, make sure you explain to her that you've been spending time on an uncomfortable bike seat before you start telling her about how sore your bum is in answer to her question.

For our last couple of days, The Bloke and I hired a car so we could get ourselves to Mossman Gorge, the

Daintree and Cape Tribulation for some exploring. And before we went home to Melbourne I bought a honeymoon souvenir: a little owl carved out of rose quartz. The Bloke and I love owls. We're no bird-nerds but we're pretty excited about the fact that we have an owl living in our street. The Bloke has named the owl 'Graham' because whenever we see Graham he just sits there and doesn't say much, which is pretty much what all Grahams do.

The Bloke is obsessed with inventing little life scenarios for Graham the owl – every time we see him, The Bloke comes up with a bit of news from Graham's life. For example, last week one of Graham's kids did their ankle at soccer training and the week before that, Graham's brother-in-law, Chris, got arrested for up-skirting on the tram. Occasionally it's amusing. In any case, because we see Graham so often I always associate owls with The Bloke and our little house, and rose quartz is meant to represent unconditional love. So that explains my honeymoon souvenir purchase. Now, let's all have a drink!

Sigh. Honeymoons are the best. It's like being in another world. And the amount of free stuff you get when people find out you're honeymooning is phenomenal. Not only did The Bloke and I get free sparkling wine from a flight attendant but he also gave us a couple of bottles to take away. Which is highly illegal, but also totally cool. On our odyssey through the seafood restaurants of Palm Cove and Port Douglas, we scored four free desserts and our beers were 'on the house' from the little waterfront café we visited. Twice! Seriously – tell all your yet-to-be-married friends that if they want to save money on their next trip with their boyfriend they should buy matching gold bands and tell everyone they're honeymooning. As long as they canoodle constantly, everyone will buy it.

When it comes to your honeymoon, you don't need me to tell you where to go (although if you cut me off in traffic, I'll happily do so). However, the following tips might come in handy for your honeymoon planning:

- Start planning and saving for your honeymoon as soon as you start planning your wedding.
- If money's tight, consider a honeymoon fund instead of a gift registry. You can buy a toaster and towels anytime. Honeymoons are special and your guests will like the idea of being able to contribute to yours.
- Go lavish if you want to but don't overspend. A wonderful time will quickly turn into a wonderful nightmare when you get your credit card statement.
- If you're headed overseas, sort out your passport and any immunisations as soon as possible to avoid having to deal with them when you're in the throes

of planning the wedding. Aeroplane tickets for overseas travel should be booked in your maiden name, regardless of whether or not you're changing it. Your passport will presumably still be in your maiden name and the names must match or you won't be allowed to travel.

- Make sure your destination isn't just somewhere that *you* want to go – you should both want to go there. Neither of you will have fun if one of you has been dragged somewhere and why argue over something that's supposed to be fun?

- If either of you can't cope without being near a bit of hustle and bustle, don't think that being on your honeymoon will automatically make spending two weeks in a remote location bliss. Remember Miranda in that episode of *Sex And The City*? It's not worth it – you'll go mental.

- Plan your honeymoon dates in accordance with the time you can get off work – don't book anything until you've had your leave approved as some travel and accommodation agencies don't refund.

- If you can't go on your honeymoon straightaway at least try to spend one or two nights somewhere else within a few days of your wedding. It could be a nice hotel or maybe simply a friend's holiday home – it's just nice to be able to surround yourselves with the nauseating stench of newly-married love.

- Unless you're super-duper organised, consider not leaving for your honeymoon immediately after your wedding. The Bloke and I had two days before we went on ours and we were glad we did because we didn't feel rushed off our feet before we left.
- Depending on where you go, combined flight and accommodation packages can save you money. These are offered through travel agents but airlines often offer them as well. And don't forget to add up your Frequent Flyer points if you have them.
- A travel agent is an excellent resource for professional travel advice (duh). Many will give you fabulous advice over the phone – you don't necessarily have to actually book with them in order to gain from their experience. And if you can't be arsed organising your own travel, they can take care of everything for you (for a fee).
- Tell everyone you're on honeymoon. Look for ways to drop it into conversation and consider having T-shirts printed. Travel and accommodation upgrades, free food and drink, discounts, improved service – all these could be yours.
- Make a special honeymoon purchase. It doesn't have to be anything expensive: just something you can display in your home to remind you of the time you spent together.

PART

FOUR

Cocktails

FOR WHEN YOU'RE TIRED AND EMOTIONAL. PLEASE INDULGE RESPONSIBLY

Martini

50 ml Bombay Sapphire Gin
Dash of dry vermouth
Green olive

Pour gin and vermouth over a pile of ice in a tall mixing glass, mix and allow to chill for a few moments.

Then, hold the ice back and pour the alcohol into a martini glass.

Spear an olive with a toothpick, drop the lot into the glass and serve.

Alternatively, chill the entire bottle of Bombay, pop in one of those bendy straws and serve immediately.

Mojito

50 ml Appleton Estate Golden Rum
5 sprigs fresh mint
2 dashes sugar syrup
Dash fresh lime juice
Crushed ice
Soda water

Place mint, rum, lime juice and sugar syrup in a tall glass and muddle with a bar-spoon until the mint stinks.

Add some crushed ice and stir until thoroughly mixed, top up with soda water and serve.

Alternatively, slosh some rum, some mint, some lime cordial and some lemonade into a glass and get stuck in.

Champagne Cocktail

25 ml St Agnes Brandy
1 white sugar cube
Angostura bitters
Dry or vintage bubbles

Moisten the sugar cube with the bitters and place in the base of a champagne flute.

Cover first with the brandy and then with the bubbles and serve.

Alternatively, pretend the bottle of bubbles is a bottle of Bombay and follow alternate instructions for Martini. Enjoy.

PART

fIvE

Relax! Things could
be worse

I'll be straight with you: There will be times during the planning process when you'll feel stressed. There will also be times when things won't necessarily work out exactly how you want them to. It's easy to let these times get you down, which is why it's so important to relax, because things could be worse. A *lot* worse . . .

Good Wedding Transport

Bad Wedding Transport

Really Bad Wedding Transport

Good Wedding Dress

Bad Wedding Dress

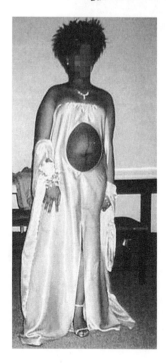

Really Bad
Wedding Dress

Good Wedding Cake

Bad Wedding Cake

Really Bad Wedding Cake

A FINAL WORD
A FAREWELL TO NEARLY-MARRIED ARMS
(AND LEGS AND OTHER BODY PARTS)

So now that all's been said (by me) and done (by you), I guess this is the bit where we say farewell.

I hope you've found my book helpful. At the very least I hope you've had a laugh and made good use of the cocktail recipes.

I also hope that planning your wedding doesn't cause you too much stress. Think of it this way: I planned a wedding despite the fact that I still can't figure out how to set the clock on our microwave. So if I can do it, so can you (and if you understand the workings of a Sharp 1100-watter, kindly drop me a line).

If you're prone to getting worked up, allow yourself one meltdown and one meltdown only. It may actually yield amusing results.

For example, I allowed myself a meltdown during the planning process and I kind of think it was justified. I mean, I went from a lifetime of thinking I never even wanted a wedding, to one day finding myself huddled on the couch with my head in my hands going, 'The guest list is too big! The celebrant's name is Barry! This whole day's going to be like *My Big Fat Greek Wedding* meets Talking Boony!'

It was while I was having that meltdown that The Bloke sat down next to me and started giving me a back tickle. You know when someone draws little shapes and squiggles on your back with their finger? And I'll never forget what he said while he was back-tickling: 'Hey, you don't need to stress. No matter what happens our day will be perfect because we'll be married at the end of it. In fact, the only thing you need to worry about is the fact that I just drew a big dick and balls on your back.'

And to think that this guy will one day father my children.

Have a wonderful wedding and a deliriously happy married life.

Now, let's all have a drink!

AcKNowLEDGEMENTS

Strap yourselves in, people.

For giving me the opportunity to achieve a dream and become a published author: thanks to my fairy book-mother, the magical Alison Urquhart, and the powers that be at Random House.

From my somewhat limited understanding, it's not often that an author reaches the end of the editing process and says 'Was that it?', so for making it all so quick and painless: thanks to my editor, the fabulous Chris Kunz.

For all her hard work, great ideas and for sharing my enthusiasm towards shifting some units: thanks to my publicist, the ever-ready Annabel Rijks.

For her unbridled joy at the prospect of this book being published and for her beautiful wedding photographs (both on the day and on these pages): thanks to the delightful Robyn Slavin of Robyn Slavin Photography & Design.

This book began as a Melbourne International Comedy Festival show called 'Terri Psiakis Has Pending

Nuptials'. Were it not for that show, there would probably not be this book. Therefore, for all their help with my show: thanks to my dramaturg and friend Catherine Deveny, my publicist Hannah Watkins, my tech Nikki and my front-of-house wrangler Tom, and all at Token Events, Token Artists and the Melbourne International Comedy Festival.

As well as being based on a show, this book was also (clearly) based on my wedding. Therefore, for all the services they provided for the big day, which in turn helped lead to this book, thanks to: Shane McConnell Couture, Jacqueline Kalab at Another Skin, Robyn Wernicke at Small Space Jewellery, Lisa Feleppa, Dina's Floral Passion, Lochiel Treetops, Wally Soltys, Livia Fontana, Rodney Swart at Tatra Receptions, Caterina Panay at Fusion Dance, Andy McClelland and Katrina Jones at Kat's Cakes.

For all their professional advice, help and hard work over the years: thanks to all at Token Artists, in particular Kevin Whyte and Erin Zamagni. Thanks also to Emily Fuller, Janine Eckert and especially Veronica Barton for helping make this book happen.

For their support, encouragement and for attending all those shows: thanks to my family and friends, new and old. For motivation from the very beginning and for continued friendship: thanks to Adele Morice.

Thanks also to the good writing vibes of the little house on Griffith Street, Port Fairy and to Chris Dalwood, for whom I always hoped to someday write a book.

Finally, to my Kingy: thank you for the inspiration and for letting me keep a notepad and pen beside our bed.